People First

People
First
The Third Federal Way

MARC A. STEFANSKI

Forbes | Books

Published by Forbes Books, Charleston, South Carolina.
Member of Advantage Media.

Forbes Books is a registered trademark, and the Forbes Books colophon is a trademark of Forbes Media, LLC.

Printed in the United States of America.

10 9 8 7 6 5 4 3 2 1

ISBN: 979-8-88750-007-2 (Hardcover)
ISBN: 979-8-88750-008-9 (eBook)

Library of Congress Control Number: 2024909319

Cover and layout design by Lance Buckley

This custom publication is intended to provide accurate information and the opinions of the author in regard to the subject matter covered. It is sold with the understanding that the publisher, Forbes Books, is not engaged in rendering legal, financial, or professional services of any kind. If legal advice or other expert assistance is required, the reader is advised to seek the services of a competent professional.

Since 1917, Forbes has remained steadfast in its mission to serve as the defining voice of entrepreneurial capitalism. Forbes Books, launched in 2016 through a partnership with Advantage Media, furthers that aim by helping business and thought leaders bring their stories, passion, and knowledge to the forefront in custom books. Opinions expressed by Forbes Books authors are their own. To be considered for publication, please visit **books.Forbes.com**.

Dedication

Life is a gift, one that cannot be taken for granted and should be lived to the fullest. I hope this book can be used as a guide, not a god, to help you live a happier, more fulfilling personal and professional life. It's no secret that one of my favorite movies is Frank Capra's, *It's a Wonderful Life*. The story parallels so much of my own life, and taught me to never underestimate the difference that one person can have on another. This book is dedicated to the people who have helped me have a wonderful life—my family—as they have always had the biggest influence on me:

My late wife, Rhonda, who dedicated her life to me and our children.

My daughter, Ashley Williams; her husband, Jamie; and their children, Sienna, Kevin, and Olivia.

My son Kyle; his wife, Julie; and their children, Oliver and Zoë.

My son Brad; his wife, Kara; and their children, Saylor and Luka.

My son Alex and his wife, Natalia.

My daughter Melissa.

My wife, Vanessa, and her children, Scarlett and Briggs.

Thank you for your love, encouragement, and support. You have given me such a wonderful life.

Acknowledgments

I want to acknowledge the following people, without whom I wouldn't be the person I am today.

- My parents, Ben and Gerome Stefanski, who were partners in business and life, but parents first.
- My brother Ben II; his daughter, Tina; and her daughter, Bridget.
  - His son Ben III; his wife, Heather; and their sons, Ben IV and Luke.
- My brother Floyd; his wife, Kathleen; and their daughter, Amanda.
  - Their son Brian; his wife, Christina; and their sons, Bennett and Jackson.
  - Their son Gavin; his wife, Jill; and their children, Archer and Milly.
  - Their son, Evan, and his wife, Rachel.
- My sister Hermine Cech; her husband, Joe; and their son Jay; his wife Julie; and their sons, Jens, Anders, and Madsen.
- My sister Gail Stefanski.

In addition, I would like to acknowledge the support of past and present board members and trusted advisors, including Bernie Kobak and Paul Stefanik, Mark Allio, Dan Weir, John Ringenbach, Bill Mulligan, Bob Fiala, Tony Asher, Marty Cohen, Barbara Anderson, Terry Ozan, Meredith Weil, Marc Byrnes, Ned Hyland, Tony Visconsi, Terry Bauer, and Kurt Karakul.

I would particularly like to acknowledge Jennifer Rosa and Cherie Kurlychek, and all of the Third Federal associates who have been the foundation of the company's success.

Lastly, my deepest gratitude and appreciation for Cathy Zbanek. Without you, I would never have been able to write this book.

Contents

Preface

All that you can take with you is that which you've given away.

That's one of my favorite quotes from *It's a Wonderful Life*; it's the motto that's hanging up in the office that belongs to Jimmy Stewart's character, George Bailey.

It's not the kind of quote a person might expect from a banker, real or fictional. People tend to think of bankers as being driven by material things—asset size, capital ratios, and growth.

This material drive is especially what people might expect when they see the success of Third Federal as a thrift. We've grown continually, retained our customers across generations, aided our communities for decades, and expanded across the country since the time Third Federal was founded by my mother and father in 1938.

But the material things are just the start of what makes Third Federal actually work. I wanted to write this book because of the immaterial things that have made my journey as a leader possible —our values, great life experiences, the help of my friends, and the love of my family. I want to honor the communities that have been built up alongside Third Federal and to share the points of view and concepts that have enabled our success.

I also want people to know how impressive the story of Third Federal and its associates is. And that we measure our success in ways that aren't always recorded.

Joe Ehrmann, former NFL star and current president of the InSideOut Initiative, a foundation focused on youth success, argued that we should measure our success against what we've given to others. It's pretty close to the way George Bailey thought. How good of a father are you? How good of a mother? A brother? A friend? What did you give away to make things better around you? Those are the things that will make your legacy matter. Those are the ways you measure success.

The values this book will focus on are all, in one way or another, ways of giving ourselves to the world. They're also, not coincidentally, the reasons Third Federal has had great material success. I want people to know that both things are possible.

The Third Federal Values

Love—a genuine concern for others,
our fellow associates, and customers.
Trust—faith in the people and their decisions; a belief
we will do right by our associates and customers.
Respect—listening to ideas and opinions,
looking to one another to make ourselves better.
Excellence—dedication to doing the best job we can.
Fun—taking the time to have fun at work.

Values, Family, and Business:
An Introduction

We Are Family

—SISTER SLEDGE (1979)

The Third Federal story really starts with my father, Ben Stefanski. Not when he started the bank, but many years before that, when he worked as a real estate secretary and managing officer at Pyramid Savings in Cleveland. My father was moving through a promising career when the stock market crash of 1929 happened, and Pyramid became one of the many financial institutions that failed.

My father was, like many, out of a job. Prospects were grim for everyone, including the depositors at Pyramid, who had lost their savings when the bank collapsed. While Dad could easily have shrugged and walked away from the depositors, he did not. Living with his mother and taking no salary, my father took seven years to make it right with Pyramid depositors who had been affected by the crash. As Pyramid struggled through its recovery, my father spent the Depression years toiling over every single customer account, no matter how big or small.

By collecting mortgage payments when possible and selling off property when he could, he eventually paid every penny back to Pyramid's depositors.

"A hundred cents on the dollar," he used to say, which meant that he intended to mark and repay every last cent, to piece back together every dollar he'd been entrusted with.

Looking back now, it doesn't escape me that this is the plot to *It's a Wonderful Life*. A good man is caught up in the collapse of a bank and then strives to pay back the depositors at great personal cost. My father was very much the real-world version of Jimmy Stewart's character, George Bailey, decades before the film even existed. Like Bailey, my father's ethical convictions were so strong that he went to every effort to repay the Pyramid depositors.

My father's attitude toward his depositors back in the Pyramid days and his drive to treat his depositors as if they were his own family are still alive in the values of Third Federal. They're the foundation upon which the now multigenerational bank has been built. After my father had paid back all his depositors, he founded Third Federal Savings and Loan.

Third Federal Savings and Loan, which we will call Third Federal throughout this book, is a $17 billion thrift founded in 1938 in a predominantly Polish neighborhood in Cleveland by my father and mother, Ben and Gerome Stefanski. The bank has prospered because it embodies the sort of respect and integrity my father showed throughout his career. Sticking to these values has earned the trust of our customers and made a family out of our associates. Third Federal was so central to the lives of my parents that they actually applied for its charter in Washington, DC, while on their way to their honeymoon in Bermuda, the business plan in tow alongside their vacation luggage. During my tenure as chairman and CEO of Third Federal, I've come to realize the importance of love and empathy, of mutual respect for everyone in the bank, its community, and its customers.

This book discusses the nature of leadership and explores how each of our core values has created the amazing, prosperous culture of Third Federal. To this end, building upon my father's legacy, we have instituted the core values of love, trust, respect, commitment to excellence, and fun into the way we run our business. This book begins with a reflection on how these values have combined to create the prosperous, built-to-last culture of Third Federal.

Our values have resulted in astounding growth, perpetuated healthy families among our associates, and re-energized many of the communities we serve. We believe that work should be gratifying and fun while also believing that all these values lead to a commitment to excellence.

These values create a positive feedback loop that not only makes Third Federal a stable, prosperous company for its associates but also one that helps its community and finally often makes a great impact upon the families of those who work and bank there. This book is meant to showcase these values for those not familiar with Third Federal and also to serve as a celebration of the Third Federal values for its associates and its customers.

The values we practice and the relationships we build at the bank have ranked us among the *Fortune* 100 Best Companies to Work For and placed us on other Best Places to Work lists many times. The more than one thousand associates working at Third Federal appreciate the values that inspire them at work and also readily apply to their personal lives. Our philosophy is one that sounds simple but that actually requires a great deal of thought and awareness—building great relationships internally and with our customers will lead to being profitable to the benefit of everyone involved. When we enrich the lives of our customers and our associates, everyone prospers.

To understand how we enact our thinking in a concrete way, it makes sense to start in the workplace. Third Federal is a bank, after all.

Our first conviction, one that I'll continually expand upon throughout this book, is to make sure that everyone wins. When our customers win, we win. We price fairly. We accept or reject loan applications quickly—a customer will know where they stand if they apply for credit. We keep our application process transparent. We keep mortgage rates low enough and savings rates high enough so that customers are attracted to us. Our business prospers based on pricing and on the incredible service our core values allow us to provide.

We call our employees *associates* to eliminate a sense of hierarchy and set the tone for how we interact with one another while at work. When we evaluate our associates, we focus on the social interactions of their relationships. Do our associates feel respected? Do they feel like their voices are valued? Their expertise trusted? We expect respect to be earned, but we also give each other the time and space to earn that respect.

This sounds simple. But it isn't. It flies in the face of what most businesses are pushed toward—exploitation of the product or the customer for maximum profit to the expense of the relationship and, ultimately, at a cost to customer satisfaction. Often, business interactions have a mindset of domination. Many think of a typical business relationship as being a competition: "I succeed if the other person fails."

This worldview is just a sour frame of mind. A person does not need to make their neighbor fail in order to succeed. We aren't yanked down when we offer a helping hand. In fact, the person we helped up might, in turn, help us up in the future.

I think often about a proverb I learned from a builder who was making modifications to one of our locations. She was impressed by the way we treated our customers. I told her it was common decency. She told me, "Those we climb over on the way up are the same people you must face on your way down." This is true but only if a person chooses to deal with others as a series of obstacles. Human beings aren't obstacles; they aren't rungs on a ladder. If we don't climb over each other, we can meet on equal ground and prosper. The synergy of treating each other right makes us work better. At Third Federal, 1+1 can sometimes become 3.

This analogy holds up in real life, as well. A 2008 study by Maslach and Leiter found that associate fatigue, burnout, and job dissatisfaction are caused by corporate focus on the bottom line. The authors claim that most employees who suffer from burnout hold very common perceptions of their organizations they work in—perceived lack of control, lack of fairness, values that do not match those of the associates, a lack of recognition, and poor work relationships.[1]

Third Federal is set up to avoid these feelings. The tables in Third Federal are round whenever a room allows it. Our lunch tables and conference tables make our associates and customers able to face each other with no one at the head of the table. To top this off, we have a rotunda and a circular courtyard at our Corporate Campus. The circle reminded the knights of the round table that they were equals—even the king didn't take the head seat. This environment makes sure that we are ready to hear each other, that we can share ideas without preconceived notions about station and power dynamics. The knights were a family who, when they were at their best, worked together. The whole thing only fell apart when they began to get selfish.

Before that, they had Camelot.

---

1   Christina Maslach and Michael Leiter, "Early Predictors of Job Burnout and Engagement," *Journal of Applied Psychology* 93, no. 3 (2008): 498–512.

It's amazing how observing our values of love, in the form of genuine concern for each other, and respect naturally leads us to collaboration instead of competition. This way both sides in a discussion win, and we don't have to damage our relationship to attain some sort of an imagined dominance. Another thing about values—when customers are aware of our values and know that we are committed to them, it builds trust.

This direction wasn't a decision Third Federal undertook in just one day. Our values are an evolution that began with my father and continues with myself and all the current-day associates at Third Federal. As we began the process of emphasizing our core values while running our business, the process wasn't intuitive. We all had to focus daily on keeping the proper perspective. We'd tell ourselves, and anyone who would listen, that observing our core values of love, trust, respect, commitment to excellence, and fun would work in a business setting and even in our family lives. And it did. As one of the largest banks in Northeast Ohio and with half million loyal customers in twenty-seven states, Third Federal's success shows that the values in this book can and will build up a business. This process took the associates at Third Federal decades to perfect, but today we incorporate our core values into our everyday life like a well-oiled machine.

We use these values to shape our operations every day. When we evaluate our associates, our service to our customers, and our leadership in the communities we serve, we are constantly asking ourselves if every aspect of our business meets the benchmark of our values. It's a constant effort, but it's worth it. It shows in every happy customer and happy associate. Like the proverbial happy cows, we make more milk.

Bringing Our Values Home

Over time, we began to find that many of our associates were not only using our values at work but were also taking the ideals of Third Federal home to their families and seeing positive results. One of the memories that really drives this reality home for me came in the form of a note I received from an associate as he retired. The loan officer's health was failing due to multiple sclerosis, and by forty-six, he was pretty much limited to his home on disability. He had been a hardworking associate. As a loyal family man and a people person, he had been a perfect fit at Third Federal. For all his years of service, he'd exemplified our values. In that letter, he wrote the following:

> I literally cried thinking of leaving Third Federal. Besides my wife and kids, Third Federal was the best thing that ever happened to me. Marc, I have always wanted to say thank you, but didn't know how, until now. Your company, as well as your family, has touched my family more than you may know. The values your company taught me, passed down from your parents, were invaluable to me.
>
> You see, I used the Third Federal values to help raise my children to who they are today. My daughter is now a great mother to our first grandson. Our son has grown up to be a 3rd class Petty Officer on the USS Nevada Submarine in the Pacific.
>
> I was talking to him last night about how proud we are of the man he is becoming. He surprised me by saying he wouldn't be who he is without the values I taught him. He said he learned respect from the way that I talked about the company I so loved, Third Federal Savings and Loan.

I always thought I was teaching good values, but as a parent you just hope it sinks in. Marc, to know the values your parents started are still alive today in our youth, is a tribute to your parents, you, and your entire family.

His sentiments shed light on why taking the harder, fairer route that the Third Federal Way represents is worth it. If the culture of a business is good enough, it might even benefit the families of those who take these values home. They're the values that make human beings both kind and good at what they do.

Work Shouldn't Be a Balancing Act

So, why do so many famous business leaders miss the boat when it comes to their family lives? Likely, it is because profit and ambition shout louder than values. Those well-known and, ironically, well-respected business leaders quit listening to what is most important. They choose not to make an effort to connect their inner business drive to what is good for their coworkers, for their community, and for their families.

The story of a billionaire who on their deathbed wishes they'd spent more time with their families is almost a cliché. But clichés are just truths that have become widespread enough to be cemented into our collective knowledge. Many people simply devote too much to workplaces that only emphasize productivity, profit, and product. Workers arrive too early and leave too late. They are in constant communication. It isn't a model that leads to a healthy life.

Most would agree that top executives have to be able to think about the future for their businesses to continue to prosper. Ironically, it is often devastatingly true that many leaders, as they focus on the future, choose to sacrifice living in the moment when it comes to their personal lives. Even more off target is that the futuristic thinking of overly consumed business leaders is consistently praised for being heroically innovative. Financial wisdom and futurism are not the keys to personal success. Yes, their companies may have succeeded, but their families lost out on the much more noble, private moments that build up true contentment, reinforce joy, and make life genuinely happy.

Our society spends a lot of time discussing work-life balance, but many leaders don't realize that business and family success can complement each other. A healthy family structure is something a person knows they can rely upon for support. A family knows that it will collectively fulfill the responsibilities and obligations that keep it functioning. These are the same principles that can make a business not just successful but also healthy in the long term.

Working for the good of your family by taking a personal interest through giving your time, energy, and care usually fosters gratitude and cooperation. It is self-perpetuating, a positive feedback loop. Good work reinforces a fundamental human drive toward helping others, according to scientific research. Even toddlers have the instinct to care for others and be concerned for the well-being of their family.

Even in the most difficult circumstances, say, grieving for the loss of a spouse, a child, or a parent, we're usually intent on supporting our other family members who are dealing with that same trauma. This sense of community helps us recover even as our family helps us. This is also true of a business that functions like a family; our desire to support each other can make us capable of shouldering the burdens of an economic slump or a tough project.

We've found that working within our enriched corporate culture, which is intent on promoting positive values and fostering relationships, also strengthens our associates' families, which, in turn, fortifies our business, our customers, and our communities. As our retired loan officer described in the aforementioned letter, this makes Third Federal something truly special.

What our associates hold dear is that Third Federal is the kind of workplace that doesn't force them to sacrifice family for career success. In fact, our core values add to their families' well-being, in part, because their careers aren't exclusively devoted to profit, ambition, or recognition but to caring about others.

Let's admit that even happy families can be pretty funky, especially when it comes to bridging generations. For example, there's that planet our teenagers go to where no parental advice seems to register with them. It's my experience that if you stay steady, you'll eventually find that they appreciate your ideas and the values you've instilled in them.

Two of our associates, a mother and a daughter, went through this very process, and Third Federal was the place where it happened. The daughter emailed me a note describing how her mother had wanted her to work for Third Federal and had tried for years to get her to join the bank. The letter went on to describe how, for quite some time, she'd been adamant about not working with her mother. Eventually, the daughter of this associate did come to Third Federal to work. Subsequently, her associate's own daughter began to have serious health problems. She went on to write:

It has been a very long road to recovery, and it has left us with many medical bills. She is finally doing well so I just keep my fingers crossed that it stays like that! In the beginning when I first found out, Third Federal Human Resources reached out to me right away and put me in touch with Rhonda's Kiss,[2] who then provided me with assistance funds to help with some of the medical expenses.

I cannot even begin to tell you how much I appreciated that. There are no words to explain what that meant to me, I really don't think there are too many companies out there that would care that deeply about their associates. Third Federal has definitely been there for me every step of the way!

I often say that parenting is a thankless job. You can't lose, you can't win, and you can't quit. But over time, it is incredibly gratifying. I'm grateful that this woman was aided in her job as a parent by being part of our family. This story is important to me because it emphasizes that Third Federal isn't a place that demands you sacrifice your personal life (including being a parent) for the sake of a business. It's a business that better enables you to live your family life. Our values give us the leadership, resources, and structure that make this possible. I love the song "Beautiful Boy (Darling Boy)," which John Lennon wrote for his younger son. In the lyrics, Lennon points to where satisfying family life can be found—by being present. Lennon sang: "Life is what happens to you while you're busy making other plans."[3]

Many of us are distracted by our planning, our work, and our hopes for the future, and that can make us miss out. Our leadership and our values try to make it so Third Federal isn't a place where that happens.

---

2   Rhonda's Kiss is a charity named after my late wife, Rhonda. I'll go into detail about its history and endeavors in "Making a Difference: A Legacy of Love."

3   John Lennon, "Beautiful Boy (Darling Boy)," track 3 on *Double Fantasy*, Geffen, 1980.

Distraction

I find that an oft-retold Buddhist tale perfectly captures how corporate culture so often emphasizes the wrong aspects of their business and how this mistake undermines why a business should exist in the first place, which is to sustain and honor the people we love and care for.

The Princess and the Crypt

A young prince was married to his beloved princess, and a year into their wedded bliss, she died. He had her buried in a silver crypt in a small garden, and he made sure that there were roses planted around the crypt. This had been her favorite. And each day as he gazed out from his palace, he remembered her when he saw the blooms. Over time, the prince decided that the roses might look even more beautiful if he were to plant some willows. Then he dug a pond to reflect the sky. He planted willow trees and instructed his servants to add fish to the pond. At night he stared into the water, and he barely noticed that he was thinking about the beauty of the crypt instead of his lost bride. As the memorial shifted into a beautiful garden, people came from across the land to see it. They sat and slept and played.

One day, years after the princess's death, the prince sat looking at the lovely garden, awash in flowers and revelers, and thought, "Only one thing is spoiling this."

He ordered that the crypt be removed. Over time, nobody, even the prince, remembered that the garden was ever a sacred place that held his wife.

The crypt in this parable is a symbol for our values. It emphasizes how focusing on these values is incredibly important. The beautiful garden is a metaphor for today's fast money, new products, fame, and the self-satisfaction that distract us from the values that really matter. If we allow ourselves to forget our values, we lose our original intention and purpose. We need to remember what's most important in life and how we can work to sustain those things. I truly came to understand this, and the importance of keeping these values in focus, when I became the leader of Third Federal.

Our values are all about creating an organization that is devoted to both selflessness and prosperity. We can be devoted to these things at the same time without losing focus on either, and the Third Federal Way is one of the paths to creating a business that provides more for an associate while also giving them the cultural tools to do more for themselves and their families.

I Wasn't. Then I Was

Much of this book is about how the core values became an integral part of the leadership at Third Federal. As an introduction to these values, it's important to examine the way our leadership style led us to these values. My dad's heart attack was, unfortunately, the de facto succession plan for the bank, which really took effect when he subsequently suffered a series of debilitating strokes.

A critical moment in my journey to finding the values of Third Federal came when I was asked to step up as the CEO of Third Federal. I wasn't in charge, and then the next moment I was.

For all of us at the bank, the absence of Ben Stefanski was sudden. At this point, my father was in his eighties. The transition was inevitable, but it still left a massive void that needed to be filled. A large responsibility had dropped upon my shoulders. Expected or not, I felt the weight of it.

I was in my early thirties when I became head of a living organism with hundreds of hardworking people's lives directly dependent upon me. Many thousands of other people's homes and savings, billions of their dollars, were now my responsibility. Meanwhile, our community, Slavic Village, a proud enclave just up Broadway Avenue from downtown Cleveland, was increasingly rudderless—suffering due to drugs, human trafficking, and absentee landlords.

There was a right way to look at this sudden responsibility. Third Federal was a unique, thriving financial institution with my father's personality written all over it. That was good because he was a good man. The management team members were good people, too. So were our customers and the local community leaders. That was a great place to start, but it shouldn't be just about the bank's performance and profit, I thought. There should be more. Make it mean something to people. Improve their lives. Touch their hearts.

The thing is, I never really sought to be a banker. It is a Stefanski family occupation, so I knew the fundamentals, even in my youth, because of my father's and mother's dynamic examples and their hard work. I like to work hard, too, but I know that not everything comes down to hard work, bootstraps, and elbow grease. Working with people with respect and humility matters as much as working hard does.

I also wasn't sure initially if my leadership style would create the same success as my father's did. I certainly knew that I would be a different type of leader. I shy away from the command-and-control idea of leadership my father had mastered. I am not always the smartest person in the room. As a result, I often feel humbled by the loyalty and commitment of people who surround me. I find humility in the work I do. Unlike the more archetypal leadership styles, I am comfortable in expressing myself using love (manifested as care and concern for others) along with our other values. I am very easily influenced by people with good hearts. I seem to attract them. This also means that I care about the thoughts of others—sometimes for better, sometimes for worse.

My father, at the same time as being a personable guy with a glowing smile, was a person who had survived the Great Depression. This made him a leader who, contrary to my leadership style, wanted to handle the business of the bank himself whenever possible. He felt that he knew the business and that he couldn't necessarily trust anyone else to know it as well as he did. This makes sense—like many in his generation, he'd suffered real loss in his lifetime. He'd grown up stuffing newspaper in his coats for extra warmth as he lived in a home without insulation. He knew how cold the world could be, and he wanted to make sure that he, and his compatriots, didn't suffer like that again. This could also make him seem monolithic and a bit distant from his employees. He felt he had to keep himself a bit removed to make the tough choices.

This isn't to say that my father didn't have strong relationships. Many Third Federal customers felt they knew my father personally. He was always around the bank. He was active in the community. He was often directly involved in negotiating their loans and in approving their great mortgage rates. Thanks to him, Third Federal customers understood the feeling of knowing and trusting their local banker.

In 1987, his memory was slipping, and that meant the structure of the bank was going to change after losing its central figure. In her later years, my mother, Gerome Stefanski, had become a larger presence in the bank's operation, but her priorities had shifted to taking care of my ailing father. My priority, therefore, needed to be Third Federal.

As I took over, I knew that anxiety was the prevailing feeling among the longtime associates at Third Federal; it's not easy to watch someone new take the lead, especially so unexpectedly. One counterbalance was to be open about my thoughts and what I saw as being best for the organization. It was time to expand the bank beyond my dad's dominant personality. I told the associates that I was determined to make my mark as CEO in my own style. Since my natural inclination is to build and enjoy trusting, caring relationships, I wanted to make people the bank's focus, as well. To begin with, the bank would need to remain stable and profitable.

Several associates had been side by side with my dad since the 1950s and had become smart, steadfast managers leading Third Federal's growth. They were still working hard when I took over, but they had heard what I said about "my own style." One of them was known as "Mr. Inside," because he had overseen operations for decades under Dad's leadership. And another was called "Mr. Outside," because he had spent years nurturing a polished sales approach with real estate brokers and builders, and he was usually involved with most of our loan applications. These two gentlemen were like family to me.

They came to me and offered to retire when I assumed leadership of the bank. What they "heard" in my comments on leadership was that I would have a "change agenda." They wanted to allow me free rein to pick my new management team unencumbered by their opinions. After listening to their presentation, I told them if they seriously wanted to retire, they could do so. Then I let them know that they had been instrumental to the bank's success during my father's tenure and that I planned for them to continue to play a big part at Third Federal in the future. I made sure they understood that I loved them and respected them—that I had always considered them to be like uncles—and that I wanted them to stay because there was still so much I could learn from them. In truth, at that time, I couldn't have run the bank without them. They knew how to keep the business rolling.

There were a few things I wanted to address as I transitioned into my position as head of the bank. The computer age was well underway in banking, and we were not at the forefront. And we needed to create a digitized personnel system. Those were two areas for us to improve, for sure. More important, Third Federal was a pleasant-enough place to work, but I wanted it to be fun and inspiring, as well. The challenge was to hold on to my dad's unshakable leadership while also building these new ideas into our culture.

We knew we could use changes in our culture to change the turnover rate at Third Federal, which was 50 percent, a number that was high for the era. We've since drastically reduced our turnover rate, averaging under 5 percent, in comparison to other financial institutions, which are typically around 23 percent as of 2022.[4]

Those qualities we wanted to instill in our culture really point to a purpose that supersedes profit. It takes continued focus to instill a genuine culture of caring within Third Federal. But once it's embraced throughout the company, it's amazing to see how, when we put people first, financial performance will follow.

It didn't take long for these goals to morph into the slogan "People first; strategy second."

I ascribe to the idea that work can be poetic, that having a good job is a great privilege. At Third Federal, finding satisfaction in your

---

4   Crowe.com, "Crowe Consultation and Benefits Survey Highlight," Crowe consulting, 2022, https://www.crowe.com/-/media/crowe/llp/widen-media-files-folder/2/2022-crowe-bank-compensation-and-benefits-survey-highlights-cfs2304-003b.pdf.

work is not a strange concept. Working hard should be and can be productive and rewarding, meaningful and maturing, enriching and fulfilling, healing and joyful. Many feel valued for their ability to contribute. Those who have lost their health know the privilege of being capable of work. Work has meaning beyond earning income.

Before the turn of the millennium, we invited a team of consultants into Third Federal. The specific details were the least important part of their report; what ultimately matters is the gist of it: Third Federal's way of operating by building caring relationships, first and foremost, is succeeding, but it is so unique to its culture that it really requires that a business embrace the same values as Third Federal to be able to replicate its success.

The somewhat stumped expression on the consultant's face still makes me laugh. Indeed, we are succeeding. Third Federal is one of the largest banks in Northeast Ohio and does business in twenty-seven states across the country, and I know that what we do here can and should be imitated—not just as business philosophy. This book is the culmination of an effort to try to inspire people to embrace love, trust, respect, commitment to excellence, and fun as values in both their personal and their professional lives. Our values allow us to make a difference on both the organizational level and the individual level, and when we keep to them, we can do more than we imagine.

The Starfish

A little boy walking down the shoreline came across hundreds of starfish washed up on a resort beach. They were a hopeless, tangled mob, grasping at each other helplessly as they tried to make their way back into the surf. The boy stuck his plastic shovel into the sand, surveyed the scene, and then began to pick up starfish and plunk them into the bucket. He waded out up to his knees and dumped them back into the sea.

An older man walked up and, after watching the boy for a moment, said, "I don't think you're going to be able to make a difference, kiddo."

Without pausing, the boy bent down, plucked up a rusty red star, and hurled it into the safety of the ocean.

"I made a difference to that one."

Adapted from *"The Star Thrower,"* by Loren Eiseley

One person can be the savior who throws you back into the water. An organization built around being that hero can make a huge difference for everyone. I've had many people act as my rescuers during my life, and I've acted as a rescuer for many others. There are problems that can't be solved by hard work alone; some problems require the assistance of others. Sometimes you're the starfish who is being rescued by a savior, and sometimes you're the little boy, and you are making a difference—one starfish at a time.

Leadership

Ain't No Mountain High Enough

—MARVIN GAYE AND TAMMI TERRELL

My mother, Gerome Stefanski, was very much a conformist. She went to church, made sure to be a good neighbor, and stayed in good standing with the community. In the 1960s, her patriotism seemed unwavering. John F. Kennedy was the president, and she was a Catholic, after all.

Things began to change when Kennedy was assassinated and Lyndon B. Johnson took office and almost immediately intensified American involvement in the war in Vietnam despite signals that Kennedy had intended to draw down.

Sometimes life presents itself in a dramatic way and creates situations that truly test our ethics. The modern world presents this as much as great moments in history—consider the recent reality of the COVID-19 pandemic and the personal choices people made during this time. My mother was someone who found an important moment in her time and stood up.

She was the stable person who held our family together and maintained our traditional, all-American family. This very stability became a conflict for her as the Vietnam War took shape and became a quagmire that sucked in more and more young American men as we watched it play out on television each night.

As the war raged on and escalated, she became horrified with the images that were being beamed home from the jungle. It became clear to her, despite the rhetoric of patriotism and the dangers of a Communist domino effect, that this war was complex and perhaps even pointless. And as I approached the age of the draft, she ruminated on the fact that her son might soon find himself knee-deep in such a war.

This came to a head one evening in our living room. She flicked off the television mid-report, turned to look at me, her face serious and calm, and said, "Look, Marc, you're not going to Vietnam. You'll go to Canada before you'll end up there. … It's an unjust war!"

It was clear I had no say in the matter. It was a heck of a surprise to me. This was my mother, who kept a date book, who was deeply proud of America and the people who served her, but here she was telling me that I'd break the law if things fell a certain way.

It was a moment that truly made me think. Until then, at sixteen, I'd basically been oblivious to such serious matters. My mother, through the force of her convictions, jogged me a bit further forward on the path to growing up in a single moment.

I had to wonder what had made her so intent on possibly breaking the law, even to the point of leaving the country. It made me think about life and death, about responsibility and morality.

At the time, I thought this was totally out of character for her. I hadn't expected her to be so firmly against the war. Many people were, but they weren't cut from the same conservative cloth as my mother. It was counterculture stuff back then from a lady who usually lived very firmly by the US government's rules.

Mom proved to be a leader in her own life and in her own family.

What do you do when what the world asks of you conflicts with what you know to be right and good? Do you follow along with what's expected of you, or do you break tradition, even if it earns you some doubt and criticism?

My mother showed me that the better choice can be to break away, even if it has a cost. She undoubtedly would have followed through on her declaration to me if push had come to shove for me or my older brother. It, perhaps, would have earned her the scorn of her neighbors or doubt in her values, but that wouldn't have mattered to her. My mother knew her own values, and she chose to abide by them, even when those values conflicted with the widely accepted standards of others.

Ultimately, my mother showed me in that moment (and in many others) what it truly means to be a leader. This might seem like an odd statement, but she did what a leader must do—lead with their conscience and do what seems best even when it flies in the face of accepted norms. This came straight from her heart and from reminding herself what was truly important to her—more important than the (in this case) arbitrary guidelines of the system.

Leading with the Heart

Many people see a chapter on leadership, and they think of management skills, which is not at all what leadership truly means. Management involves specific skills: logistics, finance, human relations, and all those different components that are where talent and skill are needed to organize and run an organization. Dwight Eisenhower wrote a letter to his son in 1943, and in this letter about the qualities of leadership, he wrote about dedication, sincerity, fairness, and good cheer. These are human qualities, the qualities of integrity and character. They aren't qualities taught in business school. If you don't like people, if you don't respect people, if you think you're better than other people, or if you don't treat people with dignity, you cannot be, in my view, a successful leader.

The heart is always involved in leadership—caring for people is the soul and spirit of influence and guidance. This kind of leadership wasn't new to my mother, not really. It was a deeply held philosophy of hers, and it just took me some time and maturity to see it. When I used to go to her office at the bank to visit with her, she'd say, "Marc, use your position to firmly guide with kindness and understanding."

Kindness manifests in leadership when your starting position is one of love and empathy. A leader needs to try to give those they lead what they need to thrive. Understanding means being open to perceiving the reality of who you are leading. What challenges are they facing? What are they capable of? What are their strengths and their areas for growth? Her mandate that a leader be firm makes it so that kindness and understanding have a place to thrive. A leader must know when they need to set guidelines and expectations and to make sure that they know when to stay the course. Firm, kind, and understanding leadership allows prosperity, and it nurtures the people who rely on a leader.

After many years as a leader, I can definitively state that my mother was right. Nurturing works.

In addition to nurturing, I think leadership involves being one who shows the way. A leader is somebody who is looking to the future, and I think leadership (as opposed to management) is more about the heart than the head.

As a company, Third Federal uses its vision of leadership to provide a sense of continuity and to perpetuate a culture in which it is easy to thrive. Our practices support our goal of using values to build relationships.

It is important that leaders listen with true empathy, trying to understand the context of a situation emotionally as well as intellectually. In his book, *The 7 Habits of Highly Effective People*, Stephen Covey writes that the key to communicating as a leader is to seek to understand first and only after that to seek to be understood.[5]

The strongest, best impulse toward leadership is love (in the sense of a genuine concern for others), which is our first value at Third Federal. The best leaders want to lead because they care about the outcome and not just to leverage strength or profit. This caring concern for others is what really makes people flourish as individuals—it's beyond any industry bubble or social domination that makes a company successful by making your associates happy in the workplace. If a company has a concern for others in its soul, it will flourish under the influence of its associates who are practicing those very values internally and with their customers. Ultimately, the actions of that company will help people to be content, keep society healthy, and make the business itself profitable.

Without values like love, business leaders find that the stakes of going against the grain of common expectations are too risky. It takes extreme confidence to test the mettle of our own thinking—all the while fighting the tendency to float along with the conventional. A leader is usually weighing the morality of what their organization does against the practical needs of their organization. The morality, something a leader must pay attention to, comes from knowing others.

When leaders show personal interest, have integrity, and embrace the value of love, they take action on the behalf of people. They have the opportunity to give of themselves and to make an effort for others' well-being. Caring—that's the true joy of leadership and also a way to

---

5   Stephen Covey, *The 7 Habits of Highly Effective People* (New York: Simon & Schuster Ltd, 1989).

make life's challenges easier to bear. A leader visits their associates in the hospital; they're aware of the family situations of those they interact with frequently. They learn about the goals and hopes of their cohorts.

Compassionate leaders help maintain balance when their associate is dealing with personal despair, such as supporting a family through the terminal illness of their mother or comforting an associate who has learned of the sudden death of a child. Although they exist now, in the 1980s, there were no academic studies that led Third Federal to apply to this sort of leadership. Just compassion and humility. You do the best you can to offer support and comfort. By doing so, others are encouraged to do likewise. If your associates see that you care for them, for what they care about, they are likely to carry that to their own work, their own leadership. When an associate runs into hard times, it's not uncommon for their colleagues to aid them in any way possible, including collecting donations or helping each other in their personal time.

More often than not, our meetings at Third Federal start with a discussion of how the lives of our associates are going. The leaders in our organization need to know their associates. The associates need to know each other. I attended a small Midwestern college where you couldn't walk across the campus without encountering a dozen people who knew you well. I try to instill this spirit in Third Federal, and then I try to encourage that spirit in the way our associates interact with our customers. This, I believe, is the reason we still exist and thrive today while many other financial institutions have struggled.

The care and empathy our leadership shows toward our associates let them know that they can trust us. This, in turn, makes the associates give more to Third Federal because they know the leadership is committed to them. It's something that could work in most institutions so long as the leadership is willing to commit the time and their personal investment.

A Slavic Village Basement

Not long after I took over as CEO of Third Federal in 1987, I hired a human resources expert whom I'd met when I previously worked at another institution. I asked him to begin with a thorough charting of Third Federal's meager personnel standards and for him to then use it to weigh the performance of our associates. I wanted to gather this information in light of our need to move the bank into the computer age. Eager to force the bank forward by letting go of some of the "pen and pencil" associates, he glommed on to a number of associates' comments about one particular associate. This associate was a longtime colleague who simply could not get along with anyone.

Jack Welch, the former CEO of General Electric, became well known in the 2000s for segmenting employee personality types. And he recommended taking quick personnel action when their business personalities become evident:[6]

- High performers who buy into the corporate culture— promote and empower them as much as possible.

- Low performers who don't buy into the corporate culture— fire them as quickly as possible.

- Low performers who buy into the corporate culture—give them a second chance in a different position to see if they can be an "A" player.

- High performers who don't buy into the corporate culture— do a public hanging where you fire them and then discuss with other managers their shortcomings.

---

6   Jack Welch and Suzy Welch, *Winning* (New York: Harper Business, 2005).

My outside human resources expert embraced Jack Welch's philosophy. He was intent on letting the associate go as part of his developing a Third Federal human resources action plan. This was discussed, and he could not understand why I was hesitant to make a personnel decision which he saw as obvious. He didn't fully understand how we apply our core values at the bank: love, trust, respect, commitment to excellence, and fun. Compassion dictated that I shouldn't let go of an associate who had worked loyally for Third Federal for a long period simply because they didn't fit the dynamics of a 1980s improvement plan.

The next day, I invited the human resources expert into the basement of our old bank headquarters at 7007 Broadway Avenue. This was a Slavic Village basement with none of the niceties of suburban basements. It was musty, creaky, and dirty down there. After descending, I pointed to the gray cinder block walls that supported the bank above, saying:

You see the foundations of this building? Third Federal wouldn't be here without these foundation walls, and we can't just simply get rid of them because one person might say that they're ugly. We don't tear down a wall because it might need a better coat of paint.

The people working here might present a challenge to our improvement plan, but they are more important than our need to modernize quickly. Our foundation is more important than a fast change. We can work around what we have because what we have works. It will just take a little more time and effort.

The associate in question, the one who inspired my basement speech, continued working for Third Federal until her retirement, never knowing of the near miss she had encountered. The human resources expert? He also stayed until his retirement and became a close family friend, too.

Third Federal has never laid off an associate due to belt tightening. Having the right kind of associates working in our business is absolutely necessary to make "people first; strategy second" more than just pretty words.

Ultimately, the tough strategy Jack Welch espouses makes sense until you go down into the basement of your own company and see who, really, has been holding up the building for the past few decades. For Third Federal, this reinforces the absolute importance of hiring people who want to work in our culture—and not everybody does, which is why we are extremely careful in our hiring. We don't want to realize after hiring someone that they are low performers and, more critically, that they don't buy into our values.

So before we hire, that's the right time to embrace Welch's guidelines. But when dealing with our associates and our customers, it's best to remember that they're people with feelings. And that those feelings of respect, empathy, and an expectation of excellence make it so that every associate has the chance to make a positive change.

Another Brick in the Wall

The key to having the style of leadership Third Federal has is to be hard on issues while being soft on people. I can almost hear the more cynical reader scoffing at this idea. How can a business thrive on being "soft"?

Such a question (and the accompanying cynicism) is part of what prevents many leaders from successfully leading their company to finding a way to becoming a nourishing, stable enterprise. The problem is the way we choose to frame the business world almost from the outset.

We don't teach our leaders how to establish the kind of stability that comes from leadership based on a genuine concern for others—a leadership that includes accounting for happiness, respect, responsibility, or accountability in both oneself and in their associates.

To this end, I'm often asked to speak to colleges, and I find that classroom ethics discussions are usually law oriented and not human oriented. This leads to schools churning out cold-eyed business grads with sharp pencils and even sharper outlooks. They've learned how to leverage technology and tap into data science, but they've also, either directly or indirectly, learned to skirt as close as possible to the unethical with these great tools and intellects. Their idea of success is, unfortunately, advancement at someone else's expense, and they will walk over anyone if there are profits in the mix. You'll rarely find someone who has been taught that a leadership based on relationships is the element that might build a company that prospers in both the short and long terms.

Implicitly or explicitly, many companies tend to rely upon negative reinforcement—the threat of cutbacks, overtime, and sacrifices to save the project. They rely on fear. It all reminds me of an ironic placard one of the human resources leaders at another company had on her desk: "The Beatings Will Continue Until Morale Improves." The sentiment might be funny in a grim, ironic way, but it's also important to remember because it's an accurate description of operating without compassion, of what truly amounts to cutting any employee who has appeared to outlive their usefulness or removing services as a cost-saving measure. It's a plague upon many businesses, and it's a race for short-term returns at the expense of long-term profitability.

This isn't a new phenomenon in terms of running a business— "commerce without morality" is what Mahatma Gandhi called it back in 1925 when he published his tract "Seven Social Sins."[7] A lack of morality in the actions of a business, something that ultimately leads to greater discord in the future for the sake of immediate profit, is a social sin. If a business leverages every sharp edge possible, it's often to the detriment of its employees and its customers, and perhaps even the broader fabric of the business itself. Planned obsolescence, heedless outsourcing, cutting corners on quality, and focusing on image rather than outcome can certainly make a person money. They also needlessly spread suffering and sow bitterness. A business with amoral leaders will often find itself filled with disloyal employees, a revolving door of disappointed customers, and nowhere left to go once it has exhausted its various cynical strategies.

When I speak to business school classes, I tell the students the truth: that their studies will likely have little influence on what makes their businesses long-term successes. As an illustration, compare these two lists:

---

7   Mahatma Gandhi and Göran Greider, *Seven Social Sins* (Strängnäs: Tragus, 2007).

TOP COMPANIES LISTED IN THE 2022 FORTUNE 500:	TOP COMPANIES LISTED FIFTY YEARS EARLIER:
1. Walmart	1. General Motors
2. Amazon	2. Exxon Mobil
3. Apple	3. Ford Motor
4. CVS Health	4. General Electric
5. UnitedHealth Group	5. Mobil
6. Exxon Mobil	6. Chrysler
7. Berkshire Hathaway	7. US Steel
8. Alphabet	8. Texaco
9. McKesson	9. IBM
10. AmerisourceBergen	10. Gulf Oil

The education of a student would have, until recently, likely focused on utilizing every manufacturing and HR edge possible, including some of the more unsavory tactics I described earlier. Clearly, US manufacturing has suffered. No number of executives with MBAs could stop that trend; no business tactic meant to lead to maximum efficiency or cost-cutting could prevent this. The natural law is that things tend to change, that no trend can be exploited forever. Fifty years of corporate entropy is revealed in just a glance at the two lists. Only one company, an energy company, has survived the industrial era to remain in the top ten.

A leadership that inspires spirit and excellence—the things they don't teach in business school—creates something that survives. Truly effective leadership in this style leads to employees who are willing to change with the times, who aren't disposable. That care transfers to loyal, satisfied customers who stay with a company through change.

All of these lead to both personal and financial success. I wish the students were taught this truth early on. An education that focuses exclusively on leveraging advantage eventually fails. The stability a compassionate leader offers, however, can endure.

Many might balk at this idea and feel as if emphasizing kindness and understanding is impossible, but one of the greatest minds in business strategy, Stephen Covey, backs this notion.

Everyone Can Win

Many are trapped by the attitude that "there is only so much pie to go around, and if you get a big piece, then there is less for me." But things change when we see life as a cooperative arena, not a competitive one, when we convince our heart and mind to seek mutually satisfying benefits in all human interactions. "We both get to eat the pie, and it tastes pretty darn good!" Stephen Covey devoted an entire "habit" to this win-win concept in his book *The 7 Habits of Highly Effective People*. He correctly saw that a scarcity mentality—the short-term view that there won't be enough to go around—was an enemy of cooperation and generosity. To fully embrace this, a leader might need to realign the way in which they view the world. A leader needs to be able to embrace what others see as a paradox.

The same idea exists through history. Early twentieth-century author F. Scott Fitzgerald admired paradoxes. He wrote, "The test of a first-rate intelligence is the ability to hold two opposed ideas in mind at the same time and still retain the ability to function."[8] It takes effort to maintain this attitude in the business world, where everyone else is thinking it must be one way or the other. Similarly, the Romantic poet John Keats believed that one was best addressing life when they could hold opposing concepts in their work, a process he called

---

8   F. Scott Fitzgerald, *The Crack-Up* (New York: New Directions, 1945).

"negative capability."[9] With a narrow point of view, life can easily seem like a series of conflicts. Instead of narrowing our view down to see an and/or situation, one should instead see the whole that these apparent conflicts represent. Greatness requires embracing concepts that others might see as opposites.

The Daoist symbol of the yin-yang represents this concept. To the untrained eye, it might appear to be two opposites that have achieved a balanced division, each of them occupying half of their universe (the circle in which they are depicted). People often misinterpret the sign as being one of balance, of reinforcing duality. That's not the case. If a person looks closely, and is willing to see what might be opposing forces as part of a whole, they can grasp the true meaning of the sign. The two forces inside the circle are actually in motion, swirling together to create an equilibrium. One drives the other. On top of that, each of the forces has a small piece of the other inside of it, as depicted by the little dots of white or black in its "opposing" force. This symbol is a whole, an ecosystem, and a person who is willing to look at the universe with this example will be able to see unified continuity where someone with a limited mindset will only focus on one part at a time. A leader can really prosper by seeing the whole rather than getting lost in conflicts that only seem like conflicts because of a flawed perspective.

In opposition to these concepts, business strategy often embraces a scarcity mentality. Many leaders are ineffective because this scarcity mentality causes them to try to grasp at temporary profits of exploitation over a more permanent state of generalized prosperity. This is emphasizing only part of reality. The secret to creating a lasting success

---

9   John Keats, *Private Letter to Brothers George and Thomas Keats*, 1817.

for a company is to embrace both the need to profit and the need to create stability for a community and its associates.

Jim Collins explores a similar thought in *Built to Last: Successful Habits of Visionary Companies.*[10] Collins examines how business dealings usually devolve into thinking of the world in terms of "or." The traditional, "efficiency-minded" worldview is that an individual can serve their community and their customer, *or* they can make a profit. A bank can be profitable, *or* it can have low interest rates and few service fees. Collins refers to this as "the tyranny of 'or.'" An individual or company that has embraced this mindset can't live with two seemingly contradictory forces or ideas at the same time. This limits the ways in which they can pursue profitability. If they deal exclusively in the "tyranny of 'or,'" companies must choose A or B, but not both.

In this same model, Collins explains how the more visionary companies of the world deal with reality on an "and" basis—embracing the "genius of 'and,'" where they think openly and recognize that there are a myriad of paths to success and numerous ideas about how to navigate them. Embracing the "and" means a business can pursue profitable endeavors while simultaneously creating a stable institution. A company doesn't need to solely pursue profit; it can pursue other endeavors while also being profitable.

Consider how the people who take action in desperate situations often describe their mindset afterward. Most think that a person is either brave enough to act or they are too fearful. They embrace "the tyranny of 'or.'" Those who pull someone from a burning car or intervene in some crime on the street don't usually describe things this way. They weren't braver than anyone else; they just acted despite their fear. Basically, they were afraid *and* they acted.

---

10   Jim Collins and Jerry Porras, *Built to Last: Successful Habits of Visionary Companies* (New York: Harper Collins, 1994).

The ability to hold multiple ideas in one's mind is important in every facet of life. While, admittedly, their situations were more desperate than someone engaging in a business endeavor, both Vietnam Prisoner of War Vice Admiral James Stockdale[11] and concentration camp survivor Viktor Frankl[12] have said that when they were up against it, they had two simultaneous thoughts in their minds: the reality of their torture and the hope for their rescue. Both thoughts were necessary to their survival, they said, so they focused on both. The motivation of what was possible once they'd escaped made them able to deal with the present. Had either of these men become too focused on the dire situations in which they found themselves, they would not have survived. They had to hold both the idea of future happiness and keep the wherewithal to survive the day-to-day reality of their struggles.

In the more mundane world of business dealings, the same is true. Treating people with compassion and earning a profit don't have to be two conceptually different ideas. They can be kept in mind at the same time. As a leader focuses on values, relationships, and profit, they might encounter what seem to be paradoxes when the matter of profit arises. Are we going to shy away from these seeming conflicts or reorient ourselves to view them as great opportunities?

Third Federal has a very low turnover rate, under 5 percent, while remaining profitable. This has remained true even during crises like the 2008 mortgage crisis and the COVID-19 pandemic. These numbers are because we've embraced these ideals. Our leadership embraces the concept of the "and," believing that we can be both profitable and compassionate.

---

11   James Stockdale, *A Vietnam Experience: Ten Years of Reflection* (Stanford: Hoover Institution Press, 1983).

12   Viktor Frankl, *Man's Search for Meaning* (Boston: Beacon Press, 2006).

Wealth Is Health

None of this is to say that Third Federal doesn't emphasize profitability. An emphasis on profit is needed to balance out compassionate leadership.

The emphasis Third Federal has on helping its various communities does require a steady and clear vision in its leadership. Leadership in this style needs to balance being soft on people with being hard on issues. I remember one particular meeting where this came to the forefront. I noticed that a number of leaders among the Third Federal associates were excitedly discussing expansions to the programs we had going on at the time. They wanted to step up our commitment to Slavic Village, the neighborhood around our original location and current headquarters. The discussion was almost exclusively based around charitable endeavors, which were being discussed with more and more exciting chatter as the meeting went on.

When my turn to speak came, the room looked at me expectantly, surely thinking, because of my emphasis on community, that I would crow happily about the ideas they were presenting. Instead, I stunned the room to silence when I simply said, "Wealth is health."

It was a twist on an old saying they were all familiar with, one that my father used often—"Without our health, we have no wealth." I'd reversed it. I could see my associates were puzzled.

We'd recently built a $30 million complex in Slavic Village. We'd led and participated in dozens of community programs. We all agreed that we'd continue to go far beyond the call of duty and foster deep relationships with the community, but, I added, this wasn't an area we could focus on to the exclusion of everything else. I meant that I was completely committed to profitability, and this needed to be fully understood by everyone at Third Federal.

I said, "Look, this is an 'and' proposition. We're committed to community and values and profits. That's in our mission statement, but we know it is a paradox for a financial institution in a capitalist system. Our job is to manage the bank around this paradox with our eyes also on Third Federal's financial health." Our goals of maintaining high capital ratios and an expense ratio as close to 1 percent as we can could not be ignored.

The meeting attendees, our C-suite executives and our leadership, couldn't be focusing on assisting the community to the exclusion of profits. We were only going to make progress as an institution if everyone in the meeting (and the groups they represented) became "and" thinkers.

As human beings, we need to breathe to survive, but breathing is not our sole purpose. The same holds true for a company. Companies need profit to survive, but profit is not its sole purpose as an organization. Customers, associates, communities, and social issues are all influenced by companies and what they provide. A leader knows that these things aren't in opposition; they are actually part of a whole.

Champions

Because we are a leader in the community, Third Federal often responds to big social events or important moments. In 2016, the Cleveland Cavaliers, our hometown NBA team, won the championship, and the community, as well as Third Federal, was euphoric. We developed and publicized a celebratory offering.

When I came into work the Monday following the final game of the series, we worked out a way to offer a mortgage purchase discount of one quarter percent. On Wednesday, I drove to the recording studio, but not our usual downtown one because there was no way to navigate through the victory parade throngs. We came up with a radio ad that ran right away.

We actually ended up extending the offer because of the response. Life was great! When the people in our community celebrate, we celebrate. We even had a championship parade in the halls of Third Federal. Our leadership has made it so that we share in the triumphs of Third Federal customers and our associates. Such an offering took what might have been a momentary blip and made it into a way for someone to make the memory permanent in a home loan. Our leadership creates a positive feedback loop that enhances both our profits and the lives of our customers.

The Wisdom of the Dalai Lama

Leading a bank with thousands of associates and hundreds of thousands of customers or leading a philosophy with millions of devotees isn't a vocation that everyone can expect to have. While this position offers a certain perspective, being a leader certainly isn't the only way to come across true wisdom. It isn't a position where one should just start passing down edicts and orders. The true benefit to having these leadership positions is that they provide a platform for helping others to understand where true happiness can be found. The Dalai Lama himself said as much in his 2001 book *Ethics for the New Millennium*[13] when he acknowledged that he looks at the office itself as unimportant. The important aspect of the office is the ability to place the influence of wealth, numbers, and a large organization to work in bringing something to the world. He used his leadership to make leaders of everyone.

Similarly, I can review the early days of being CEO of Third Federal and see how my vision for the bank has become a reality, in part, because the bank's associates were eager to follow their CEO's lead of building great relationships and putting values into practice.

---

13   His Holiness the Dalai Lama Tenzin Gyatso, *Ethics for the New Millennium* (Boston: Riverhead Books, 1999).

Consider what the Dalai Lama discovered about leadership positions and true happiness:

> [They] contribute not even a fraction to my feelings of happiness when compared with the happiness I have felt on those occasions when I have been able to benefit others. ... Actions we undertake which are motivated not by narrow self-interest but out of our concern for others actually benefit ourselves. And not only that, but they make our lives meaningful.[14]

The Dalai Lama said narrow self-interest and the pursuit of material things often lead to frustration and anger, drives that are the enemy of happiness. Those in wealthy countries are especially caught up in the idea of constantly acquiring more, so much so that it takes up every moment of their lives. The constant need makes happiness essentially impossible. The Dalai Lama points out that this moment-to-moment absorption can make us little more than animals if it is our only impulse.

A wise executive must see the danger in excessive concern with a "have-it-all-now" business strategy, at the expense of building relationships. It takes patience to see the long-term benefits of forsaking such a path.

Whether we are in a leadership position or not, each of us can be happy if we have a balanced view of our circumstances. Patience with the present while still having plans for the future are the dual states a leader should be able to contain within themselves. The Dalai Lama describes it in this way: "For example, there is nothing we can do about old age. Far better to accept our condition than to fret about it."[15]

---

14   Ibid.

15   Ibid.

When we work to benefit others—when we put people first, strategy second, as we do at Third Federal—our hope for the future becomes a great source of calm. It allows us to sometimes leave money on the table for the sake of stability, or to provide service above and beyond the call. We can't control the future, but we can control our reaction to the present and the way we interact with the world.

Balance

Among the multiple paradoxes a leader must confront is the very real likelihood that when things look like they are going well, soon they will turn bad. There's a colonial American saying, "Geese fly higher when the weather is good." Fair weather won't last, and there will soon be bad weather in which the same geese will have to fly low, beneath the cloud cover. There's a connected bit of New Englander wisdom: "Beware the goose hung high." This implies that even though times are currently extraordinarily good, we should act and make decisions with the view that times will change. To put it plainly, good times won't necessarily remain so good.

That was my father's view of Third Federal's capital position. When things are going strong, set aside reserves for the bad times. I followed suit by making it clear to my team that maintaining a double-digit capital ratio remained a priority for us, and that strategy got Third Federal through the tough times of the 2008 financial crisis. Still, it's hard to maintain a sense of urgency in the good times. We can't see the shape of those looming bad times, and it's impossible to predict when they'll come. Good times don't absolve us from preparing for a troubled future, though. We shouldn't be lazy, complacent, or foolish about bad times ahead. Beware the goose hung high. Celebrating the good times while simultaneously getting ready for the worse times ahead is a paradox. Balanced leaders need the wisdom and energy to maintain these two concepts side by side.

Sharpening the Saw

A reflection on leadership would be incomplete without touching on another concept from Stephen Covey, the idea of "Sharpening the Saw."[16] The analogy draws on the fact that a saw that gets used often also needs to be sharpened often or it becomes ineffective. It's the notion that, because leaders engage in so much activity and bear so much pressure, they must regularly "sharpen" themselves. There's obviously no whetstone for humans, so instead, human beings must find the activities that make them ready to engage with the world at their best. This can be relaxation, a hobby, an art form, really anything that affirms why we work.

I play music. Music is a way of sharing time with a community and also bringing others happiness. I've been playing since I was a teenager, and now I have a jam band that has been playing together for decades. We can really pack the house, sometimes bringing in a couple thousand people to hear us play. I also enjoy playing for Third Federal associates and often bring the band when we want to have a fun event (more on that in the related chapter "Fun"). At Third Federal, we value a work-life balance for our associates, which is all a part of our appreciation that we all need a chance to sharpen.

Sharpening the saw is all about reminding yourself why your leadership is important. We work to be human. The more we can make that work related to the things that matter, the better.

---

16   Stephen Covey, *The 7 Habits of Highly Effective People* (New York: Simon & Schuster Ltd, 1989).

Taking Action

A Zen master notices that one of his disciples had done nothing for several days but sit in the meditative position.

When asked the reason for this, the student replied, "I wish to become a Buddha" (acquire Buddha nature).

At this, the master sat down beside him, picked up a brick, and began polishing it with a stone. After a while, the student asked what he was doing.

"I am polishing this brick into a mirror," was the reply.

"But no amount of polishing will make the brick into a mirror," exclaimed the student.

"And no amount of sitting with your legs crossed will make you into a Buddha," the master replied.

And no amount of sitting will bring about the changes we desire. We must do something if we wish to pursue the goals we have described, goals that affect our work, our recreation, our relationships with others and, most of all, our deepest understanding of our own nature, from which springs the tranquility that we all require.

Love

All You Need Is Love

—THE BEATLES

When I was a teenager, I had a high school football coach who was, in almost every way, the stereotypical image of a rough-and-tumble gruff leader you'd see on a television show. He was a short, stocky, imposing guy who (I realized years later) looked almost exactly like an Italian World War II general I'd seen in a documentary. He looked like a man who'd taken a million hits and who always got back up, more gnarled and tough because of every lump.

Needless to say, he was an intimidating presence.

A lot of people would stop really perceiving him there and think that he was your stereotypical harsh coach—the kind of guy who barked threats and criticism and inspired you to greatness with a combination of challenges and goading—someone who demanded you earn their respect by withholding it. This man wasn't so simple.

Yes, he could be extremely tough—he saw everything that happened on the field and in practice, and he wasn't afraid to be direct and blunt about your skills, a play, or the effort you were putting into practice. Most of all, though, everything he did came from caring deeply about who each of his players was. All that attentiveness, energy, and observation came down to having a caring concern for others.

One of the times, looking back, when he illustrated this was when he put me in during the end of a blowout game. We must have been winning by thirty points, and my coach could have laid back and coasted us to victory. Instead, he started switching in people who hadn't had a chance to get serious game time. He put me, a freshman, into the game to try my hand on the field.

The stars (or more likely all of the coach's expertise) aligned and left me with a clear path through the offensive line, and I was able to complete a spectacular hit on the rival quarterback. It was so clean and devastating that I can still remember the impact and the takedown decades later.

After the game, as we were in the dark parking lot and streaming back onto the bus, the assistant coach hollered my name and yanked me out of line and over to where he and the coach were standing. I thought that perhaps I was in trouble for the hit or for some other slipup I didn't even realize I'd perpetrated. Instead, the coach reached up and gripped my shoulder with more strength than you'd think was possible.

"That was a beautiful hit, Stefanski," he said. "You're starting every game from here on out."

I sighed with relief.

Coach didn't have to put me in that late in the game, and not every coach would be observant enough to see a pattern worth repeating from that single play. That coach knew I'd perform because he loved his team. This isn't the first word people might jump to when they think of a role like this, but I've learned that leadership, teamwork, and community involve love as their values when they're at their best.

"Love" is the kind of term that gets a cringing reaction from the cynical realists of the world. It's the kind of term that might even earn someone an HR meeting in the right context. Love, in reality, defined in terms of the values of Third Federal, means a genuine concern for others.

My coach showed that love to all of our players. He was genuinely committed to making sure that we lived up to our full potential. Not just as a team but also as individuals. He paid attention to our strengths, he knew us, and he helped us with guidelines and boundaries that let us grow. He also wanted what he'd learned was best for us, and he'd learned what was best by putting in the time and interacting with our team. He cared about our goals and used that energy to great effect while still providing structure. This, in turn, manifested in the way we treated each other as teammates. His love made us a great team.

Some of this I didn't see until much later. This coach ended up being a big figure in my life as I grew into my leadership role, and the values he'd taught me eventually became part of the inspiration for Third Federal's value of love.

By the way, we won all eight games that year. We were undefeated. That synergy between a coach who cared and a team who knew it is a potent strength.

A Genuine Concern for Others

At Third Federal, love is one of our values—perhaps the value from which all our other values, in one way or another, originate. In the context of Third Federal, love refers to the genuine concern for others. It guides our organization, the culture among our associates, and our interactions with our customers. It's the foundation for our customer service, the products and services we offer, and for how we interact with our community. So how do we practice love on an institutional level, and how does that end up benefiting Third Federal and its customers?

For starters, we place our genuine care for our customers and our associates above all other concerns. This means we do not engage in short-term strategies that might alienate customers, be bad for our associates, or damage the long-term reputation of Third Federal. We place a huge emphasis on listening to customers and getting to know them as individuals so that we can best meet their needs and so that they know they are a part of a community when they are a part of Third Federal.

This genuine care we have for our customers has been so effective that we retain customers for decades and generations, and we draw in many of them through referrals. We also regularly receive letters of thanks. Both our associates and our customers tell us that they feel as if they are part of our family when they're interacting with Third Federal—that they are grateful that our organization is what it is and that they feel thankful to be a part of it. It all sounds very utopian, but it's also a practical matter. This culture centered around the value of love greatly strengthens Third Federal and has enabled us to be a multigenerational bank that is the cornerstone of the communities where we have established branches.

In addition to using love as a guiding principle for our interactions with customers, we emphasize love among our associates. We use a "walking around" management style where our managers take the time to get to know associates on the individual level. As part of this, we encourage input from all our associates. We hold town hall–style meetings to hear concerns and make sure everyone stays informed. Love, and the demonstration of genuine concern, is actually one of the first items in any associate's biannual performance review. Although it's qualitative, love is as critical to our business model as any quantitative measure. We need our associates to know each other, to know our customers, and to provide service in a way that demonstrates the values of Third Federal. We expect that our associates will take both the needs of our customers and those of other associates into account whenever possible, that they will always maintain a level of respect and empathy as they carry out their duties, and we make note when someone excels and really takes the initiative to be loving and supportive.

As a result of this emphasis, we have minimal annual turnover among our associates. We also only have a third of the associates an organization our size typically has. Our associate turnover is under 5 percent. The turnover for financial institutions tends to be much higher, typically 23 percent in the banking industry. These numbers let us transition a significant portion of our company into an online workplace almost instantly during the COVID-19 pandemic, and it kept our workforce intact through it all. People at Third Federal are willing to go the extra mile for our values.

Having a loving workplace leads to strong financial performance for the bank. Our customers sense our commitment to them and see in our actions the importance we place on knowing them and thereby meeting their needs. This means they use the products we suggest, they trust us with more of their money, and they know we will provide them with appropriate mortgage loans. They know their long-term best interest is also ours.

The financial side of our business stays strong when we address our values and don't take shortcuts to play a mere numbers game. We avoid commissions, exploitative fees, or risky ventures that place numbers above our customers. We will not provide a loan to a person who should not have it (which, as I'll discuss later, has saved our bank quite a bit of trouble). This is as much for their benefit as it is for ours.

Yes, like any other institution, our business goal is to maximize our market share in a given area. We always aim to be number one or number two in market share in our area—and to widen that gap between us and the next-best company. And we work hard to achieve that, but we also believe that this success comes from a certain management style and type of customer service rather than from looking at our customers only as a source of profit.

That effort matters to our customers. They want to interact with associates who will genuinely listen to them and care about them. They feel the love in our process, which starts with interacting with them as equals and building a relationship that manifests in skillfully handling their savings and painstakingly focusing on their mortgages. In almost every interaction, our customers walk away glad that they've worked with our associates and our bank.

Even situations that might normally be a negative interaction with a financial institution can be positive at Third Federal. A company that operates with love as a value strives to keep that value even when they have to live up to the unfortunate responsibilities that come with their industry.

Default Isn't Always Your Fault

One of the best ways to show our ideals in action is to consider our process in an area of the bank not often seen by many customers: Default Services. That's where our associates interact with customers who are having difficulty making their mortgage payments so that they can try to negotiate a payment schedule and perhaps help a customer to plan their finances to make their payments.

Because Third Federal tries to make the right kind of loans to qualified home buyers, one of our customers not making their mortgage payments may be a result of some unforeseen circumstance—the death of a spouse, a divorce, a health crisis, or the loss of employment—deeply unpleasant situations that are nevertheless a reality of life.

The best thing we can do to start this process is to make sure that the Third Federal associates answering the phone or meeting with customers who are undergoing these troubles treat them with genuine concern and respect. One of our seemingly very simple guidelines is to answer the phone with a smile. It's a simple physiological fact that if an associate smiles when they pick up the phone, their voice will convey a different tone than if they aren't smiling. The same holds true with face-to-face greetings. Our customer is already stressed; otherwise, they wouldn't be going through the default process. They should never be made to feel that they are disrespected just because they aren't currently in good financial health.

More often than not, these mortgage payments will get sorted out; that's why there's a meeting between Default Services and the customer. This is when Third Federal associates listen to what the customer is saying. Associates are trained to listen, not to take control of the conversation, but to listen with respect to the customer's feelings and anxieties. Next, with understanding, associates ask questions respectfully about the situation and if there's anything that can be done to alleviate the circumstances.

Of course, there is an underlying legal contract that will hold sway over the final resolution, but, in the meantime, our associates develop and maintain sincere empathy for the customer, which the customer can sense and which might create a circumstance where the associate and the customer are able to work out a solution, a modification, or a payment plan.

The result of this process is that we have a remarkable record of retaining mortgage customers who undergo temporary financial difficulties, and we operate under the premise that we save each home, one borrower at a time. We take great pride in our work to make all our customers successful homeowners.

Relationships Are Made
Out of Time and Effort

Building strong relationships takes time. As Stephen Covey wrote, "With people, fast is slow and slow is fast."[17]

Relationships based on genuine concern for others are not always perfectly predictable, and they take time. Building an organization based on this value takes an investment by the leadership to always put the idea of genuine concern at the forefront of our actions. It requires complex, personalized interaction in a world where many sentiments are boiled down to an emoji or a tweet. Both corporate culture and the culture of the internet encourage us to finish interactions as quickly and as efficiently as possible, but this way doesn't lead to the kind of stable, positive results we see at Third Federal.

Living life to create great relationships based on love gives us the opportunity to make something meaningful. The culture of finding meaning, of pursuing a good life, is often erroneously taken in the opposite direction. In the pursuit of living a good life, many people are advised to settle on feelings like serenity or contentment. Those are positive feelings, but they often fail the institution or the family because they are all about the self. Being content or having serenity doesn't necessarily motivate a person toward the goal of building loving relationships. One might be content to be alone, to take the easiest path. They might find serenity by avoiding uncomfortable situations, establishing a kind of artificial harmony that is ultimately meaningless. Those who take this path might miss the hidden truth in building relationships.

Taking action on behalf of others leads to success and joy, and this leads to growth and self-improvement. Love, manifesting as genuine

---

17   Stephen Covey, *7 Habits of Highly Effective People* (New York: Free Press; Simon & Schuster, 1989).

concern for others, leads to mutually beneficial relationships. A drive to help others forces a person to be part of the world, and they grow from it. Finding your motivation in helping others makes it so that a person can't just watch from a distance.

So how does this apply to running Third Federal or to any other large organization? This drive helps the engagement an associate feels with their organization. Once you've had the thrill of growing by helping others, you can feed off the excitement that comes from working to improve other people's lives in both small ways and big ways. You can find meaning in both the tangible and intangible manifestations of love that come from this kind of involvement. Happiness stems from your actions, even if you're called upon to shoulder someone else's pain or engage in a difficult situation.

In the early 2000s, Third Federal had a moment of truth where our values were tested, and we emerged stronger and did so in a way that another organization with a different set of values would not have managed. A neighborhood rights group with some very legitimate grievances had set its sights on protesting banks in Ohio. They noticed that their neighborhoods were being targeted with practices that extracted wealth from their neighborhoods, engaged in predatory lending, and then moved on from the area, leaving its people worse off than where they'd started. Third Federal was not engaging in such behavior, but other banks were, and the neighborhood advocacy group formed a corporation that was engaging with every financial entity in their area. This included Third Federal.

The goals of this advocacy group were good, but things were also contentious. They were protesting at our main branch to the extent that business shut down, and the police intervened. One of the protest tactics was also to show up at the homes of banking leaders. They were demanding that bank presidents sign a contract that outlined how they would interact with the neighborhoods they represented. Even though I could sympathize with their goals, I still had a responsibility to the goals and well-being of Third Federal, and I couldn't meet every demand in the exact way that they wanted. I knew we needed a conversation.

I did the only thing I could think of. I asked to meet with them. I dressed in casual clothing and met them face-to-face. They were people who, just like me, wanted to protect their families and our neighborhoods. I met them from a position of genuine concern—I let them know that I appreciated what they were doing and why they were doing it. I also acknowledged our differences—in race, income, and life experience. I told them I couldn't sign their contract, that it wasn't tenable for my bank, but that I would do them one better.

I'd offer a promise to do right by them and their neighbors, and I'd seal it with a hug.

I crossed the room and hugged each member of the group, letting them know I'd always do my best to treat them fairly.

They were astonished. And also satisfied. They didn't protest against Third Federal anymore. After that day, and over the years, they've used Third Federal as an example of how a bank should treat people.

We must have done something right, because now one of their members sits on our board as a director.

Loyalty, the love for our community, is something I learned from the old guard of Third Federal, those who worked alongside my father starting in the 1950s and then continuing into my leadership. Their stories went back even further than their time at Third Federal. When you talked with them and other families who had experienced the Great Depression, they'd tell you that, even though the 1930s were desperately sad, one good memory that remained with them was how people showed empathy for one another. They recalled how families put up signs in their windows saying, "Need help!" and how their neighbors inevitably came to assist them. These professional and personal relationships helped form strong neighborhoods, and the same values fostered in these neighborhoods eventually built a thriving Third Federal that helped people rebuild their lives.

This ethic carried over to the modern era of Third Federal—that very same love is what made Third Federal able to work with the neighborhood advocates. We always remember where we came from, and we strive to build an institution that succeeds because of caring and concern for our fellow humans. This helps us to last when others have failed.

Season of Life

Love is the core value of many successful institutions. Joe Ehrmann, a high school football coach-turned-motivational-speaker from Baltimore, used the value of love as a linchpin for his coaching style. This value enabled him to change the lives of his students (and many others). I read his biography, *Season of Life: A Football Star, a Boy, a Journey to Manhood*,[18] as I was figuring out core values for Third Federal, and it captivated me. It epitomized what I was searching for: I wanted Third Federal to have a cause bigger than itself, bigger than banking. Ehrmann worked as an inner-city football coach in Baltimore, where he distinguished himself through his unique approach to sports, endeavoring to have his players and their parents see the activity through the lens of love, not aggression.

Part of his practice and a ritual before his games involved the players and coaches saying "I love you" to each other to help instill

---

18   Jeffrey Marx, *Season of Life: A Football Star, a Boy, a Journey to Manhood* (New York: Simon & Schuster, 2004).

the proper spirit in which the sport should be played. Ehrmann saw the game as a way to bring others together. He wanted his players to support one another instead of engaging in a relentless drive toward winning and achievement. His book details his attempts to encourage high school football players to realize that they had been misled by a culture that emphasizes social bravado, financial income, and male dominance. These are all ideas that emphasize the self to the detriment of everyone else. A system built on love, however, builds resilience into a culture. We keep going when an individual would quit because we're intent on performing for each other, not just for ourselves.

It's an incredibly powerful book because it reveals how our ordinary association with others fuels a reserve of great strength within ourselves. We want others to thrive, and this helps us succeed together. Every player on Ehrmann's team, for instance, got a chance to play. Ehrmann and the players on the team emphasized whatever unique skill their teammates possessed. One player, for instance, was able to run incredibly fast in a straight line, but he didn't excel at other aspects of the game. Ehrmann, seeing this skill for the asset it was, designed plays built around the skill rather than benching the player because of his shortcomings in other areas. Ehrmann cared about his players, learned their strengths, and therefore built a team that won.

I could see that there was a similar need in the banking industry, not to mention society as a whole. I gave the book to a handful of associates to see what they thought. They loved it as much as I did because Ehrmann shared a lot of Third Federal values. Eventually, we actually brought Coach Joe to Third Federal to speak with many members of our management team. Many associates found his discourse to be riveting, even life changing, so Third Federal went a step further and sponsored speaking engagements for Ehrmann to present his ideas to area coaches, parents, and school administrators.

The feedback was incredible. I was thrilled with how strong the reactions were as audiences heard Ehrmann and came to understand that they were obsessed with achievement when what they really needed was to be more focused on caring for others. It is the antidote for a society that is self-oriented, transfixed by device screens, and untethered from person-to-person relationships. The institutionalizing of caring relationships as a value at Third Federal was a decades-long process, even though it really wasn't such a huge deviation from what my father had built. To this day, many customers recall their interaction with him. They tell me that they trusted him because they knew he cared—and they still trust Third Federal today.

That was the feeling that I wanted to perpetuate when I was taking over the bank in the late 1980s, and I'm glad Joe Ehrmann was there to serve as such an inspiration for me and later for Third Federal.

Manage by Walking Around

The Third Federal management team likes to walk around. You may have heard of "management by walking around." It began as early as the 1960s and was solidified in the 1982 book, *In Search of Excellence: Lessons from America's Best-Run Companies*.[19] Really, it's just a bit of terminology referring to a number of concepts that support an up-close-and-personal management style rather than managing from a distance, from behind closed doors, or from behind a computer screen.

Walking around is really about engagement, about making sure we know each other. We stand by an associate's desk for a little longer if the conversation warrants it, rather than rushing back to work. We listen empathetically. When it's warranted and wanted, I'm not above giving a hug. Business at a bank can be serious, but I never hesitate to break

---

19   Tom J. Peters and Robert H. Waterman Jr, *In Search of Excellence: Lessons from America's Best-Run Companies* (New York: Harper and Row, 1982).

out a smile. It's important to look someone in the eye, to truly engage with what they're saying and be aware that you're listening—whether the conversation is casual or about strategy. Someone engaging in the walking around style will be observant, and they'll acknowledge the accomplishments and victories of their associates. Our managers make sure their associates are comfortable discussing the time they fall short. This trust will make them willing to try again, to change, and to get into the details. Ultimately, walking around is all about the details because details are what caring is all about. We try to make our interactions face-to-face, and we do not make big decisions over email. We manage our associates by using numbers to gain perspective rather than "by the numbers," as many organizations do. We work with each associate as an individual with the objective that everyone is our favorite. This often means that one associate's output will differ from another's.

To facilitate knowing each other, Third Federal associates wear name tags. Third Federal is getting big enough that when associates from the branches, or from out of state, visit our Broadway campus, name tags are a kindness that smooths out the awkwardness that comes from forgetting names. From the customer's perspective, an associate wearing a name tag is immediately more accessible and trustworthy. It's a sign that says that an associate is an individual who is willing to be responsible for their satisfaction. They're someone who wants to get to know them by their first name.

Our management tries to lead by example by instilling the idea that problems for customers or other associates can be turned into opportunities to demonstrate care and concern by listening to them with empathy. That means listening to understand, not necessarily to respond. If a customer feels that an associate recognizes their feelings, then there's a basis for resolving problems. It all begins with our associates displaying a positive attitude, which is compelling, even comforting.

Recently, this was put to the test as we returned to the office after the COVID-19 pandemic. We did a lot of walking around, talking with our associates during this period, and prioritized the opportunity to share and address concerns. We ultimately did what was best for our common cause and our values at Third Federal, and this was possible because of our genuine care for each other and our customers.

Our company culture strives to remove a lot of the negative feelings that lead to infighting and strife inside of a company. If our associates know that their opinions, ideas, and contributions are genuinely respected, they'll be less inclined to feel the need to compete to look good. If they are secure in their positions, they won't see others as competitors but rather as collaborators. We benefit from being a lean organization, which means our associates have plenty to do and thus know that each of them is contributing to our collective efforts in a significant way. We have created a culture where we are truly happy for an associate who gets a promotion or a team of associates who receive an honor. We know each other, so we know the person who promoted them, we know how they earned this promotion, and we know that we can rely on them in their new position. Everything we do benefits our associates because that's the culture we've built.

In this spirit, at Third Federal, we frequently utilize cross-functional teams to work on projects and solve problems. Various associates bring their experiences and expertise to the table and pool them and produce far better results than they could individually. It's great to become involved in a project where each person is doing their part, not dominating the team, but contributing to a shared goal. When associates interact together genuinely, and they're open to each other's influence, the team gains insight. That's synergy.

Our expectations for our associates are very high, and we ask them to work hard during the day and to be fully engaged with their tasks, their interactions with associates, and to practice high-energy mindfulness. This is an endeavor that takes a lot of effort and intention, so it also makes sense that we do not impose on an associate's family time after that workday has ended. Family is, after all, of critical importance to our values.

We expect everyone to work hard while they are at work, but we also let it be known that getting to know each other is not a failure to work hard but is, in fact, an act of hard work because it's integral to making sure our associates have great working relationships. It's expected of our associates. Walking around also goes a long way toward enjoying one's work. Deep professional relationships add value to the company, and for our associates personally, as they make everyone stronger and more connected. The effect of our loving culture on associates working at Third Federal is telling: they are happy and loyal. The average tenure of our associates is more than twelve years, and many of our associates retire with over thirty years of service. In fact, when we celebrated our eighty-fifth anniversary in 2023, 12 percent of our associates had been with us for more than twenty-five years.

Two Cabbage Heads Are Better Than One

Despite my father not being overt about love being a core value during his tenure as the head of Third Federal, he definitely encouraged our associates to learn about each other and engage in the practice of using that knowledge and respect to be more than the sum of our parts.

Once, one of my father's oldest business partners and I stepped out from my father's office after we'd teamed up to solve a particularly difficult problem. As the door swung shut, my father called out with a saying he often used at home:

"Two cabbage heads are better than one!"

The partner turned to me, his face filled with confusion, and asked, "Did the boss just call us cabbage heads?"

I had to laugh because it's a saying I was very familiar with. It was my father's unique take on a universal truth about synergy, both at work and at home. When a relationship is working, it's as if $1+1 = 3$. When our skills add up and amplify each other, an organization that respects each of its members can be more effective than any individual.

Being more than the sum of our parts by emphasizing the value of love means that we are ready for any difficulties we face whether that's an economic downturn or a particularly challenging project. We're also prepared when an associate's personal and family relationships are suffering. We know that this is a time when their work relationships could suffer. By making Third Federal a supportive environment, a place where we care for each other and the customers, work can become a comfort during these tough times rather than a burden that must be endured while an individual weathers their difficulties.

We know each other and try to understand the personal stresses involved in our lives. We've had many instances where our associates take up collections for each other after an accident, illness, or a loss. We also support each other in our victories—anniversaries, birthdays, weddings, and births. Love in the workplace makes work a place where life is actually lived instead of just something that's completed so that a person can get by. A burden shared is half a load, as one of my directors often tells me.

I try to know our associates well. Even if I don't personally know much about a given associate, I know their close coworkers and managers will. Our value of love ensures that Third Federal tries to offer a support system for those who need it. This makes people value the institution. They contribute freely; they know that they have a future here and that their ideas are valued. This value lets us thrive.

Being "two cabbage heads" involves both accepting help and giving it. We all know that love has to be selfless to really work. Relationships are supposed to be a two-way street, but it isn't universally balanced at all times. Sometimes we're carrying all the responsibility for a time, making all the effort, in a relationship. At other times, someone else has carried us for a while. Striving toward being more than the sum of our parts, and doing this out of caring and concern, helps to keep any relationship balanced.

I've also, over the years, learned that there are times when love requires boundaries and judgment. The boundaries and guidelines of the processes at Third Federal are an act of love. As a collective endeavor, an institution shouldn't favor one person inside of it above the others. We have standards for a reason; it protects everyone. This is something I learned early on.

There are times that people with personal connections to me have asked that I step in to help them get a mortgage for which they are not qualified. It pains me, but I have learned that I must not do so. Empathy does have limits. It's a collective failure of responsibility if a person bends the rules and jeopardizes the financial health of others. Love demands that we think of the best interest of the many, even when we're inclined to be charitable to an individual. Caring and concern have to go both ways to be a functional philosophy.

Associates at Third Federal understand this. They're aware of the generosity of the organization, but they don't take advantage of it. Their care and concern extend to those who demonstrate our core value of love.

Addiction

Having seven children has taught me a lot about life and love. We must love someone for who they are and not for who we want them to be. This is something that has helped me get through difficult times. An important part of having love as a value is making sure we know what to do when people fall short of our expectations. My family, like many others, has experience with addiction—which means I have experience with addiction—because loving an addict means that everyone involved is affected and challenged.

This experience has deeply influenced having love as a value at Third Federal, and it has taught me that love is not always easy. My desire to keep love as a value also means that I have learned that I must accept reality and deal with life as it is, not with life as I wish it to be. One must learn to let go with love.

I have learned from my experience with people suffering from addiction that sometimes we have to love people as they are and accept that their actions are outside of our control. Not accepting reality, wanting someone to be what we want them to be, or wishing that we could control their behavior can lead to skepticism, anger, and lowered expectations for others. Instead, I learned to practice empathy even when circumstances disappointed me, to learn the limits of what could be expected of others when they're clearly suffering and confused.

This wasn't an easy lesson; before I learned acceptance, I was focused on my feelings of disappointment and didn't care much about what others were going through. Yet, through my contemplation amid hardships, and through the one-day-at-a-time process, I am glad to have had the experience because it taught me something valuable: to understand difficulties, especially those greater than my own. The process forced me to articulate my commitment to love and to apply my values. It forced me to grow. It helped me to love.

We should have firm standards for appropriate and acceptable behavior. Yet, if we love people for who we want them to be, then we are offering conditional love. If we love them for who they are, then our love is unconditional.

Achievement Can Be the Enemy

When I was in my early teens, my parents sent me to summer school in Connecticut. I had a blast, and I was just beginning to find a real talent for sports. When they came to pick me up at the end of my seven weeks away, I climbed into the car and almost immediately tried to show off my award for athletics. Deep down, there might have been some hope for praise, but their response was disappointing—my father pointed out that I had no awards for academic achievements or for leadership. I was achieving, but I just hadn't achieved in the way that they thought I should. Their definition of success was very narrow, and it focused on academics, not on sports.

Today, we view achievement differently than my parents did. Stability, low costs, and a strong balance sheet were the mantra at Third Federal during my father's tenure. Those are still a huge focus today, but since the mid-1980s—when we decided to make love one of our values—making a profit and building caring relationships have been the areas where we need to excel. We will always carry a strong balance sheet, but we also have a firm commitment to carry our values. Not all achievements can be made into a mathematical measurement. Striving only toward the kinds of achievements that are easily measured puts us in a position where values like love fall by the wayside.

Making our values areas of critical importance seems necessary to me. Society's culture has become addicted to money, fame, and instant achievement. There is a tacit, almost society-wide approval and acceptance and unrestrained drive toward profit and even notoriety. The stability and satisfaction of living a values-driven life show that this is fool's gold. Pursuing achievement, profit, and metrics will have only fleeting benefits—and these benefits have very little to do with happiness.

Creating strong relationships based on a genuine concern for others results in stronger, long-term performance, both on the personal level and in the business world. The only difficulty I've faced as a result of emphasizing love in my life is that I worry that some people might think I'm too positive, too nice, to be taken seriously. I doubt that this is true, but I don't mind if it is. The financial success and stability of Third Federal speak for itself. These values have tangible results.

Simply put, we show loving concern for our customers. As a result, our customers are loyal to us. And we have approximately 400,000 customers, and our retention is well above the average for a bank our size. Third Federal retains 93 percent of our customers, compared to 50 percent average retention rate in the industry.

Even technology like the internet doesn't hamper the personal connection we have with our customers, because we remain resolved to put the customer first. When our customer care and marketing teams ask online mortgage customers how they found out about Third Federal, almost two-thirds say a relative or friend recommended us. Young couples in Ohio often say their parents or grandparents insisted they come to Third Federal for their mortgages.

Working with customers creates a winning cycle. It begins with building relationships. Next, revenue and profit increases come into play as a natural result of offering a superior experience and culture. We consider profits to be a litmus test report on how we're doing with building relationships. And then the cycle completes with further investment in relationships.

So, unlike other banks, Third Federal's end goal is not solely shareholder value. This might seem like a shocking comment for a CEO of a public company to make, but it is not in any way minimizing that responsibility: I simply mean that financial metrics are not the sole factor that drives our success. Our top and bottom lines have grown steadily since 1938, and they've done so in conjunction with our commitment to our values. Because of this, our successes are fulfilling and largely a result of us keeping to our values—not in spite of them.

Everyone is my Favorite

A peer of mine once told a story that illustrates how much leadership is about caring — and how much caring isn't about hierarchy. This CEO was getting on an elevator with another executive, and saw one of the janitors in the elevator. He paused his conversation with the executive and talked to the janitor.

"I hear your wife has been sick. How is she doing?"

The CEO and the janitor had a short conversation, going on long enough that the CEO had to hold the elevator door open when he reached his floor. Then he and the executive got off the elevator, now a bit late for their morning meeting.

The CEO could tell that the executive was a bit peeved that their conversation had been interrupted and that they were now late. The executive asked him, "Why'd you bother with that? We're in a hurry, right?"

The CEO simply told him, "That man keeps this place running. If his wife is sick, it's as important as one of our wives being sick. We stick together or we fall apart."

The Ben & Gerome
Stefanski Era

*My parents, Gerome and Ben Stefanski
on their wedding day, 1937.*

My mother earned not only a Bachelor's degree from Notre Dame College, she also earned a Master's degree from Catholic University in Washington DC in 1936 (pictured), a rare feat for women during the Depression era.

My parents stopped in Washington DC on their way to their honeymoon to apply for the charter for Third Federal Savings & Loan, 1937.

My mother and her five children. Front: Floyd and me. Back: Ben II, Mom, Gail, and Hermine.

While my father's primary focus was on Third Federal and his family, he was also an accomplished equestrian and enjoyed horseback riding as a hobby.

Residents of Slavic Village come to the Third Federal Main Office on a Friday evening to cash paychecks, make mortgage payments, and deposits, all under the watchful eye of my father (standing against the far wall). He always wanted to be close to customers, who were not only depositors, but neighbors as well.

During World War II, financial institutions supported the importance of every citizen being involved in the war effort by selling US Treasury Bonds. My father (light trench, left) and residents of Slavic Village on the steps of the Shrine Church of St. Stanislaus, promoting the war bond drive.

Third Federal Associates and Community

With Barbara Anderson and Inez Killingsworth from ESOP (Empowering and Strengthening Ohio's People) accepting an award for a commitment to honest lending practices to minorities and low income areas of Northeast Ohio.

The Once-a-Month Club band performs at Joe's Crab Shack at a Florida Associate Appreciation Event. Through the years, associates and board members have joined me on stage for shows. These annual events, held in Florida and Ohio, draw nearly 5,000 associates, family members and guests for food, fun, and entertainment.

The grand opening of our new
Garfield Heights location in 2013.

As part of a celebration of its 10th anniversary
in 2017, The Third Federal Foundation
donated $500,000 to United Way of Greater
Cleveland, to further enhance its support
efforts for those in low- to moderate-income
areas of Northeast Ohio. The Foundation was
established with $55 million dollars from
the Third Federal IPO in 2007 to support
housing, financial literacy, and educational
challenges in communities the company serves.

Winter meetings are hosted annually in each region where Third
Federal has branch locations. Dinner, followed by entertainment
and my remarks, round out the evening each year.

*My nephew Ben III, daughters Melissa and Ashley, granddaughter Sienna,
son Brad, and nephew Gavin at one of our annual regional meetings.*

*In 2022, Brad and Gavin presented me
with my 40-year service award.*

*A pep rally in 2015 to celebrate and motivate associates, reminds all in
attendance of the company's 2005 motto, "Yes! We Can." We remain focused
on how associates can best serve customers and say "yes," to helping them
achieve the dream of home ownership and financial security.*

Third Federal Milestones

My mother and I are surrounded by the Third Federal Board of Directors for the 50th anniversary of Third Federal in 1988. I became Chairman in 1987.

Members of the Stefanski family at the 50th Anniversary celebration of Third Federal. Front row: nephew Jay Cech, daughter Ashley, my mother, son Kyle, aunt Genevieve Zeleny. Top row: brother Floyd, sister Gail, wife Rhonda, sister Hermine, brother-in-law Joseph Cech, niece Tina, brother Ben II.

With brothers Ben II and Floyd.

*With my older brother Floyd, at the 70th
anniversary of Third Federal in 2008.*

*With my children at Nasdaq on April 24, 2023, for the 85th
anniversary of Third Federal. Brad, Ashley, Melissa, Alex, and Kyle.*

*The board of directors, management team, and members of the
Stefanski family celebrate the 85th anniversary of Third Federal
by ringing the closing bell at Nasdaq, April 24, 2023.*

Family

Third Federal goes public on April 23, 2007.
Supported by my family on Times Square:
Kyle, Rhonda, Melissa, Ashley, Alex, and Brad.

My late wife, Rhonda.

On vacation with my family: Bottom: Kyle, Brad,
Alex, Ashley. Top: Melissa and Rhonda.

With Alex, Kyle, and Brad, at a Rhonda's Kiss
event to benefit City of Hope in Los Angeles.

With my children at the first Rhonda's Kiss benefit concert at the Rock and Roll Hall of Fame in 2015. Rhonda's Kiss was started as a charity by our family to honor Rhonda and to support cancer patients in need through partnerships with hospitals, including the Cleveland Clinic, to cover non-medical expenses, like rent, utilities, wigs, and transportation costs. Through 2023, the charity has provided more than $2.5 million to hospital partners around the US.

With my daughter, Ashley, vice chairman of the board of directors.

Youngest daughter, Melissa.

My wife Vanessa Rooks Stefanski and I at the 85th anniversary of Third Federal at Nasdaq. We have seven children and seven grandchildren between us.

Vanessa and her daughter Scarlett and son Briggs.

Second, third, and fourth generations of the Stefanski family join the 85th anniversary celebration at Nasdaq headquarters in Times Square, April 24, 2023.

"LIVE! Life is a banquet and most poor suckers are starving to death." –**Auntie Mame**

Trust

A Matter of Trust

— BILLY JOEL

On April 23, 2007, my fifty-third birthday, I rang the closing bell at Nasdaq. It was the day that the parent company of Third Federal Savings and Loan made their initial public offering (IPO). My family, our management team, the directors, a number of Third Federal associates, and I had traveled to New York City for our IPO. Our stock was priced at $10 per share, and I rang the closing bell for the exchange that day. Back at our offices, associates watched the event on TV. They held parties to celebrate the addition of public shareholders to our organization and community. It was a great day.

This would be a huge day for anyone, maybe their most memorable day ever. For me, however, the time that truly stands out is almost a month before. It was the closing day of the period in which those with priority access, Third Federal customers and associates, could buy shares in Third Federal before our IPO. The inside of the building, the outside, and the parking lot were lined with customers and associates who were holding the special white envelopes we were using for the offer.

On that warm, spring afternoon in the parking lot of our Broadway Avenue headquarters, I watched as our customers began to back up traffic on the streets in their rush to park and submit their envelopes. We started to get concerned about the safety of having so many people on the street, and about meeting the approaching deadline, that Third Federal associates went from car to car to collect the envelopes, filling up white plastic mail bins with piles of orders for immediate date stamping and processing. It felt surreal. It had taken decades for Third Federal to accrue $1 billion in capital, and now we had made $1 billion in just one day. I ran around helping to keep things moving, making sure everyone had their chance to get in our IPO. Our customers had brought in their friends and family to open accounts so that they could be a part of our first round of stock. I was absolutely humbled by the response, and humility, I've come to realize, is a key

This was also a big change for many of our customers. Generally, Third Federal customers are wary about investing their money in the stock market. In fact, some of those who took advantage of their priority access in 2007 had never purchased stock before. Despite this, that day found them lined up down to the last moment. Some of these people lived in the same neighborhood from which my dad raised $50,000 in seed money to start Third Federal more than eighty-five years ago. This moment was even more meaningful than Wall Street embracing our $1 billion public offering. Why was this moment more valuable than what many people would see as the pinnacle of a career? Because it was the result of an immense amount of trust on the part of our associates and our customers. Most of those buying the stock were long-term customers and people they brought in with their fervent recommendations. Without the implicit trust of our customers, we wouldn't have had such a massively successful priority stock sale for our IPO.

Trust is one of Third Federal's core values. It's the culmination of both the love and the respect we have for our customers and our associates. It's integral to any business, but it's especially vital to the work that we do and the company culture we've established. Since the first bit of trust my father established by paying back the Depression-era depositors at Pyramid Savings, Third Federal has made sure that we have the trust of our customers and that we've created a company where associates can rely on a shared trust to get the job done in the best way possible. This means we prize clear communication, transparent decisions, and providing customers with clear expectations for the outcomes of our customer service. We also foster the expectation that our associates will go above and beyond in their service to live up to the trust our customers place in them. Whether that means spending extra time on the phone or running into the street to fill up plastic mail bins with customer orders, we live up to that trust.

Although trust itself is a soft value, the results speak for themselves. We have a record of strength and stability, so our customers knew to believe us when we told them that the proceeds from our IPO would be used to further increase our capital position and facilitate an expansion that would make us even more stable. Third Federal had a $5 billion market cap and $10 billion in assets at the time. It currently has $17 billion in assets as of 2024. This is a result of the trust our customers place in us. Our commitment to honoring that trust is what put us in a strategic position that allowed us to survive the 2008 mortgage crisis.

When we pursue trust with customers, we start off by establishing a strong sense of mutual communication. One of the frequent pieces of positive feedback we receive is that we use "layman's terms" as we explain our loan offerings and the loan origination process. We also engage in the fastest turnaround times possible with our loan approval process and document preparation. Customers left waiting generally trust the process less and grow more anxious about what's going on with their loan. Similarly, we let customers know exactly what their rate will be when they apply. Many banks wait until the loan is being finalized and closed before offering the true rate. They want to bait and switch the customer—obviously not a move that's going to inspire trust. Ideally, our customers know what's going on throughout the entire process, and they trust us once they see that we're plain dealers who uphold our end of the relationship. We want them to see for themselves that we prosper when they prosper and that we survive by keeping them as a customer and even earning their trust and support so that they bring their families and friends to Third Federal.

As an old friend and executive I used to work with would say, "Trust is the hardest thing to gain, the easiest thing to lose, and it's great when you have it." When one has it, they need to steward it carefully. The way we conduct our business always keeps that in mind.

Commissions

As a means of maintaining our value of trust, no one at Third Federal works on commission. Commissions drive banks toward making deals that are based only on the bottom line, including giving loans to those who are unqualified. To provide a loan to someone who doesn't qualify is not caring, it's unethical, no matter how much it temporarily boosts the bottom line. Throughout the 1990s, banking was becoming more complex because of deregulation and increasing wealth in the United States. As restrictions were being removed during this period, rapid growth was expected. As a consequence, many banks were offering new products, from interest-only loans to pick-a-payment loans, and they were increasing their largely commission-based sales force.

In this environment, we felt Third Federal customers might be at risk if our loan originators operated on commission. What is best for our customers in the long run might not match a commission-driven loan originator's short-term objective. Our customers are not pushed into mortgages they don't need or can't afford just to generate commissions. Third Federal doesn't use advertising with misleading statements or quick subtext and caveats. The available rates are right up front and central. When a customer enters Third Federal to take out a loan, our associates are trained to take them through every step of the process, and we have materials that outline the process in an honest, clear fashion.

Based on our values, we felt commissions would produce greed, which is the opposite of what we have promised our customers. The trust our customers place in us demands that our motive be to lend to qualified customers, not to rack in commissions and transaction fees. For some time, especially when the culture of lending for the sake of commission was king, we had trouble hiring and retaining loan originators because we seemed "backward" compared to the rest of a banking industry that was frantically lending to anyone they could. Ultimately, though, what we offer loan originators is a long, stable career, a steady organization, and a close relationship with both our customers and our associates. Those who value working in that kind of environment are the right choice for us, and that means the extra care we take in hiring is worth it in the long run.

Our values, manifested in our attitude toward commission, saved us, and our customers, from a lot of pain. The commitment to be trustworthy made us last where others failed. During the mortgage crisis of 2008, Third Federal survived where others did not. We didn't push speculative loans to unworthy borrowers, and our loan originators had no drive to get the commission from doing so. We stayed stable with a large capital ratio, while other banks needed bailouts or folded completely. Our respect for our customers and our mission to put qualified homeowners into homes saved us.

Our values, rather than just an image, are what make us success-ful. Our values ensure that we keep a high capital ratio that keeps us strong, stable, and safe.

Substance over Style

There is a distinct difference between having character and merely having an image of trustworthiness. Plenty of companies masquerade as being trustworthy. Few of them truly are. Trust can't be something that's just touted in advertisements; the behavior of a company has to reflect that they are worthy of trust behind the scenes—especially where the customer can't see. Our commitment to not having com-mission is just one of the ways Third Federal does this. We don't operate with hidden fees, enact policies that are disadvantageous to our customers, or engage in lending practices that are unclear. Most, if not all, of the banks that folded or needed rescue during the mortgage bubble of the early 2000s had advertising that touted how they were trustworthy and stable. Their behind-the-scenes behavior indicated that they were anything but, and the market and the regulators even-tually found them out.

We live in an era where it is very easy to project a public relations image that isn't reality. Traditional media, social media, and the wide-spread emphasis on brand identity have combined to make what is and isn't real a confusing matter. Celebrities, influencers, and others project lifestyles they don't have, values they don't hold, and interests that they purport to be ethical or for the greater good. In the meantime, they are really attempting to line their own pockets or those of their cohorts. Many organizations and people have a personality that looks great from the outside but has very little substance.

It's a disheartening experience when the substance of the world turns out to be different from what's advertised, because trust is a two-way relationship, and it's something we humans tend toward. Humans are at their best when they're able to trust. We become greater than the sum of our parts when we can confidently cooperate with each other. Third Federal customers trust us with their mortgages, and we trust them to repay those mortgages. As they benefit from a loan and home ownership, they become loyal customers of Third Federal. They often bring in other members of their family or become multigenerational customers with great loyalty. We benefit from each other's trust, and Third Federal never undermines that trust—because broken trust can be quite devastating.

Honesty Is Better

One of the events that demonstrates how trust can be misused in the banking industry, and the consequences of doing so, is the Wells Fargo fraud scandal of 2016. This scandal emerged when a major bank, one of the top in the United States, was revealed to have been deliberately misleading its customers in a variety of ways. Thousands of their employees, driven by sales targets, compensation incentives, and commissions, found ways to sign up existing customers for new services they'd never asked for. They even opened millions of accounts under their customers' names without permission. The top managers of these institutions initially profited from the practice with performance bonuses until they were caught by investigative reports and, eventually, authorities. At the end of the day, bank executives did not punish their peers. Oh, they feigned contrition by publicly ending these practices, but they left bank customers as victims who had had their trust broken.

This company publicly preached trust, but secretly used their customers as a source of unethical profit. Those bank managers and employees threw away their self-respect and integrity for the sake of a quick increase in their performance metrics while trashing the bank's corporate reputation. It seems clear that there's little chance of customers trusting the bank in the near future. It's a pity, but given the emphasis on numbers and profit, not a surprise. That's why Third Federal is so careful with the trust of our customers. That's why we take great care in our interactions with our customers, maintain transparency, and avoid the commission structure that has become all too common in our industry. For more than eighty-five years, we have been building trusting relationships with our customers, and that trust is renewed every time they walk into their local Third Federal branch, call us for help, or use our online services. Third Federal is structured in a way so that our customers know we're not going to betray their trust.

Our identity is very well established. We're a conservative savings and loan that sticks to the basics and gives customers great rates. We survive based on honest prices and top-tier service. More important though, many of our customers truly know us on a personal level. They knew my dad. They know me. They know the people who have worked at their branches for decades. I'm always working on building new relationships on this level, as are our associates. I've met thousands of our customers during our day-to-day operations. I make it absolutely clear that I value their choice to come to Third Federal. I know our associates value that choice as well—and I believe our customers see that gratitude and know that they can trust us.

We leverage our years of experience and the years of trust our customers have placed in us, by putting that experience to work for all our prospective customers. Our typical customers only buy a few homes in their lifetime—we, however, transact billions of dollars of business each year as home loans. This means that we are much more aware of the unscrupulous practices out there in the mortgage industry. We provide all our prospective customers with education to under-stand the mortgage process. We developed an explanation of possible bad practices in a graphically simple format called "Borrower Beware," which itemizes areas in the mortgage process where customers need to be wary. We have placed it prominently in all our branches and on our web page because we are intent that anyone inquiring about a home mortgage—even if they go elsewhere—should be aware of the risks. This kind of action on our part shows our customers where our intentions are, and that has won us far more customers than trying to exploit them for an extra couple of dollars.

Third Federal fights hard to occupy a space best understood by a thought experiment created by Stephen Covey in his book *The 7 Habits of Highly Effective People.*[20] The premise begins with the hypothetical idea that you need heart valve replacement surgery. You hear about a surgeon whose patients absolutely love her, but as you check her credentials, you hear that some people in the know say that this particular surgeon, despite caring deeply, isn't exactly competent. She has lost a few more heart valve patients than is average. She would undoubtedly put in her best effort, but you might not make it through the surgery intact. You continue your research and track down an extremely competent heart surgeon who has credentials from all the best medical schools and years of experience. Her success rate is phenomenal. It turns out that this doctor, however, uses pig valves as a replacement if she encounters even the most minute problem. You want an artificial replacement, which this surgeon sometimes does, but the caveat is that she'll put you under and then decide which one to use based on the scenario. You absolutely don't want the risk of the pig valve procedure being used.

Ultimately, in Covey's thought experiment, neither surgeon is someone you can trust. One isn't very capable despite their best efforts. The other is likely to ignore your wishes because of convenience. To

20   Stephen Covey, *7 Habits of Highly Effective People* (New York: Free Press; Simon and Schuster, 1989).

maintain trust, you need to fall somewhere in between. You need to be capable and to accomplish your goals while also having good intentions. On the other end of the spectrum, efficiency doesn't replace good intentions or make up for taking away a customer's agency. Third Federal is successful because it maintains the "middle path of truth," a coin termed by Buddhists to describe a life path that does not use extremes. It is efficient but not mercilessly so. It honors the desires of its customers by helping qualified customers get the services they need, not the services we want to sell—and certainly not services they are not even aware of. Honoring our mission statement to place qualified borrowers in homes and adhering to trust as one of our core values keep us on this middle path.

This is a very necessary line to draw for the banking industry. Many people are distrustful of the financial industry—only a small number of people implicitly trust bankers to act in their best interest. My experience shows that even fewer people associate ethical behavior with bankers. The industry has given them very little reason to. The advertisements of financial industries have constant promises, but these ring hollow when these same institutions drive up their revenues through transaction fees, ballooning interest rates, or other deceptive practices. Customers are not dumb. They are quick to sense that bank managers are more interested in extracting some minuscule percentage point in profit by pushing more debt and adding fees than they are in caring for customers' well-being or their future as a patron of the bank. This is the kind of behavior that undermines our industry. It's the behavior that has doomed more than a few financial institutions. The Dalai Lama stated it very succinctly: "In business or money matters, if you think only of the immediate profit, then you will have to suffer in the long term."[21]

---

21   Sander Tideman, Business as an Instrument for Societal Change: In Conversation with the Dalai Lama (Abingdon, England: Routledge, 2016).

Untrustworthy Math

I grew up with two brothers and two sisters, which meant there was a variety of family cars in our Shaker Heights, Ohio, driveway. As the youngest of the five, it was my job to wash them all. And I was eager to please, especially after I started my own campaign to get my driver's license.

I was developing considerable skills in auto detailing when my mom's car fell into my lap. She had moved on from her light green 1967 Oldsmobile Cutlass to some other car that I don't even remember now. But I do remember that the Cutlass, with its V-8 engine and black vinyl top, became my car. Man, I really cleaned that car, inside and out. I mean weekly, if not more often.

I bring this up to establish the curious emotional relationships our prideful imaginations sometimes create with our cars. It is a phenomenon well known to Detroit car companies. So, it mystifies me how these same companies could sanction an ultimately unsafe car. In virtually the same era during which I was committed to my Cutlass, two American car companies seemed to me to lack the integrity to protect their customers from deadly designs.

Clearly, the leadership of that era did not care about their customers like their customers cared about their cars.

In the early 1960s, multiple companies became aware that there were technical problems with the designs of their flagship models and that the cars should not be sold to consumers. In one case, these flaws, which ultimately ended up costing the lives of some consumers, could have been fixed to be safe for less than $15 per vehicle. The companies, despite the danger to the consumers, declined to do so.

The leadership of these companies used a risk/reward analysis to determine whether the monetary cost to them of making the change outweighed the cost they would incur if a certain number of customers died. It appeared that the cost of making the repairs would be more expensive than the deaths, so the companies released the flawed vehicles.

This ended up becoming a major national news story, and the companies paid a much heftier cost than they might have anticipated as their customers lost trust in their brand and their products.

What sort of person generates such an analysis? The memory of this time looms large in my head. Third Federal will never, willfully or knowingly, be in a position where it betrays the trust of customers for the sake of a bottom line. Numbers look petty when they're stacked against what really matters. Trust, one of the best assets we have, is not something that should be played with for the sake of financial gain.[22]

Mistakes Are Different from Bad Decisions

When it comes down to establishing trust, it's important to delineate between a mistake and a bad decision. One should never allow oneself to be in the position of having deliberately made a bad choice for the sake of profit or expediency like the companies discussed previously. Mistakes can happen from a lack of knowledge, a flawed perspective, or plain bad luck. A poor decision is when a person knows all the facts and decides to act poorly anyway—whether that's for the sake of personal gain, pride, or some other factor. The mortgage crisis of 2008 is definitively the result of bad decisions. Sound financial decision-making was thrown out the window as commission-driven mortgage bankers virtually papered the country with bad loans—and the management of these banks was solidly behind their bad decisions as this played out. Heart surgeon or banker, we all make mistakes, but the source and intent of these mistakes matter. Although many

---

22   Ralph Nader, *Unsafe at Any Speed; the Designed-in Dangers of the American Auto-mobile* (New York: Knightsbridge Publishing Co., 1991).

of the main players in the mortgage crash later described their actions as "mistakes," the bulk of their actions say otherwise. The underlying greed and disregard for the customer, and for the market as a whole, speak volumes toward the fact that their actions were bad decisions. In the rare circumstance that Third Federal has a mistake or oversight, our long relationships with our customers, our transparency, and the clear influence of our values let our customers trust us enough so that we can make things right. We work hard to step up and fix situations another company wouldn't involve themselves in. When Third Federal commits to something, it commits.

This isn't to say that we don't take risks. Risks are calculated and made, but we are in the business of only taking the risks that are in the best interest of Third Federal and our customers. We won't, however, gamble on the trust that our customers place in our institution. We recognize that we need long-term trust for our value-driven model to work.

Trust Requires Follow-Through

Trust is, by its very nature, a long-term commitment. Life would be easy if things like our IPO story could could have a fairy-tale ending llike "happily ever after," but some of our customers who had been with the bank almost since the beginning, began to run into problems a few years after purchasing the preferred offering of our stock. We began to get calls from customers who had purchased stock and who had since become widows or widowers or who were the surviving family members of those who had purchased the stock. In many cases, these customers were unfamiliar with stock ownership and the disposition of their investment.

These surviving spouses or family members didn't understand what to do about the Third Federal stock that was now part of their estate. So, they called Third Federal, the institution they knew and trusted. As similar calls came in, we found that the best answer we could give was to tell them that they needed to visit a brokerage and enlist their help because we were unable to do anything for them. And this was true. We'd sold them the stock, but we weren't a brokerage, and we couldn't handle all of their subsequent stock-related circumstances. The complications only grew as our older or less experienced customers were unable to figure out how to find someone trustworthy, how to join online services, or how to even find them. We felt like our approach was inadequate. Years ago, they'd happily driven to Third Federal and had been a huge part of our public offering. They put their money and faith in Third Federal and walked away confidently. We simply couldn't bear to leave them floundering and unsure.

Unease rippled through our organization as these calls came in, so we trained associates in how to answer stock-related questions.

This wasn't an action that directly benefited the bank in a tangible way, but it was certainly the right thing to do. When a heartbroken customer calls because they trust you to guide them through uncertain times, you just have to help. It's also the kind of action that creates a lasting relationship with a customer and lets them know that they can trust your institution for generations.

Sometimes an action that takes up time and doesn't yield a direct profit is the best one. It's not only morally correct, but it also creates a genuine, lasting relationship between you and your customers. The numbers will show later—and sometimes the trust benefits you in a way that can be surprising.

Our Customers Step Up

In his book, *Leadership Is an Art*,[23] Max De Pree described an inclusive approach to trust. He said there is a synergy built into the two-way nature of trusting relationships. "Each of us is needed. Each of us has a gift to bring. Each of us has a deep-seated desire to contribute." This synergy makes us able to be more productive and act more creatively than we could ever be on our own.

The fact that we have created such a strong bond of trust with our customers gives us a strong relationship to build upon, and these relationships work both ways. Even after all the time we spent encouraging this trust in our customers, I had never fully grasped how we might someday find ourselves in the position of having to call upon that trust in a dramatic fashion.

After the 2008 mortgage crash, the legislature responded by implementing these regulatory changes, and Third Federal found itself in the position of being overregulated. Third Federal was deeply involved in negotiating its way through sweeping changes in government regulations, including the creation of the Dodd-Frank Act. In response to the mortgage lending crisis of 2008, the Office of Thrift Supervision was no longer the regulatory agency for banking, and the Office of the Comptroller of Currency was taking over bank regulation and implementing new policies. Guidance was changing so that a bank could only have home equity lines of credit with outstanding balances equal to a certain percentage of their capital. Given Third Federal's mission statement to put people in homes, variable home equity loans were, of course, a significant part of Third Federal's portfolio, and this new guidance put us out of compliance overnight.

---

23   Max De Pree, *Leadership is an Art* (East Lansing: Michigan State University Press, 1987).

There's a fair amount of anxiety someone in my position is always under, so the trouble Third Federal found itself in weighed on me heavily. Since taking charge, the responsibility of having the trust of my associates is something that's never far from my mind. I have an obligation to succeed. I have read that two-thirds of second-generation business owners lose their companies. When a son takes over a father's business, people make certain assumptions—if the business does well, the father built it well. If it fails, well, the son probably screwed it up. Needless to say, I didn't want to be that son.

This sudden swing in regulation was threatening the trust everyone had placed in me, and it was frustrating because it was through no fault of our operations, which were exceedingly honest and conservative. One day we were in compliance, and the next we were in violation of new regulations despite our strong capital ratio and solid fundamentals.

While we were in the penalty box, we were unable to pay dividends, buy back stock, or merge with other organizations. We also had more direct oversight from the government. It was almost unbearable because there was an underlying injustice to it all, since Third Federal had not participated in subprime mortgages, and yet we were about to bear the brunt of new legislation despite the fact that we were a solid enterprise with a great capital ratio. Despite this solidity, the salaries of some of our leadership had been cut by 60 percent, and our associates did not receive a bonus. So many things suddenly went upside down in the aftermath of years of greedy, self-serving, subprime lending practices that were carried out by other banks. The perpetrators were rewarded with bailouts and government capital infusions. We didn't need a bailout, yet we were the ones who were fighting for our lives, lobbying Congress. The irony bothered and disappointed me.

At this low point, we sent out letters to our customers asking that they send Congress messages endorsing Third Federal, and they responded with an overwhelming show of support. Their letters asked that Third Federal be allowed to stay in our current structure and only pay dividends to public shareholders. As a result, some five thousand letters from our customers poured into the House Banking Committee, which many on Capitol Hill regarded as a surprising number since the issues were complicated and not particularly exciting. After this, we launched another round of letters of support and made many personal visits to Capitol Hill. We created enough noise so that members of Congress finally understood our plight.

The years of our building trusting relationships between ourselves and our customers allowed them to trust us and take action on our behalf.

Weathering this crisis deepened my understanding of what it takes to be a leader in the banking industry and where Third Federal, as an entity with an established personality, stands within that industry—trusted by those who matter the most, the customers.

It also reinforced my appreciation for and understanding of our customers—and human nature in general. It showed that if I prove trustworthy through my life, never sacrificing my integrity for the short-term advantage, I can expect that sometimes others will return that integrity. If your promises are trustworthy, then—like the saying goes—your word will be your bond. Your "Yes" will mean yes, and your "No," no.

Trust is a value that has served Third Federal well. My father took on the trust of his friends and community when he started Third Federal in the depths of the Great Depression. The trust the community placed in us let us grow, and we always did our best to earn that trust and maintain it. That trust bolstered us as we expanded across Ohio and into Florida. That trust carried us through crises, to the great day of our pre-offering of our IPO to our customers, to my ringing the bell at Nasdaq and then celebrating with my colleagues and their families.

It's a value worth living by. It's certainly a principle that has made Third Federal what it is, and good principles are worth maintaining.

Two Brothers—A Parable About Trust

Two young brothers were traveling a great distance to begin their training at a monastery. The journey was long and dangerous.

Near the end of their travels, they beheld the massive river they'd need to cross to get to the monastery.

They approached a short, powerfully built, ferryman.

"Hire me to take you across the river," he said in an impassive and self-assured voice.

One brother, who was untrusting, said the man looked like a criminal and they should find another way to cross. The other brother, who was more trusting, said this was the fastest way, and that they should take the ferryman's offer.

They hired him and the ferryman guided the boat with the brothers.

As they approached the shore, the ferryman turned to them and said, "You'll have to swim from here. The water is too shallow. I'll throw your packs and cloaks to you."

The trusting brother stripped off his cloak and immediately swam to shore. Eventually, the untrusting brother did the same.

The boatman gathered their packs and looked as if he was preparing to throw their belongings to them. Then he shouted,

"There's your first bit of wisdom brothers," and he rowed away with their packs and cloaks.

When they arrived at the monastery, an elderly monk greeted them from the top of the tall walls.

He threw down two rope ladders, and the brothers began to climb. When they neared the top, the monk stopped them.

"This is a place of wisdom, young men. Before you enter, tell me what you've learned on your journey," he said.

"Trust nobody," said the untrusting brother.

"Be careful who you trust," said the trusting brother.

The monk drew a knife from his robes and slashed the ladder of the untrusting brother. He fell to the ground below.

"We often receive what we put into the world," the monk said to the brother on the ground, stifling a smile.

The untrusting brother dusted himself off and climbed the ladder of his brother. He trusted that his brother would keep the monk from cutting this one too.

Trust is what makes the world function. When it's used correctly, it benefits everyone. It's easy to lose and hard to gain, so cultivating trust in Third Federal's customers and associates is one of the most powerful forces behind our success. Whenever you can cultivate trust, do so; it's an investment that offers rich returns.

Respect

R-E-S-P-E-C-T

—ARETHA FRANKLIN

My mother was a huge influence on my belief that women in the workplace can be as capable as any man. As I was growing up, I witnessed a very strong woman, my mother, raising a family while simultaneously working hard on Third Federal matters, especially on advertising and marketing efforts. Third Federal is a family business, so bank issues were often discussed at home and often in front of us kids. We saw firsthand the sort of respect Dad and Mom had for each other. They always heard each other out on ideas and went to each other for advice and an alternate point of view. My father, despite the general attitudes of the day about women in the workplace, took my mother seriously and understood how much she contributed to the family's success.

Once, when I was just a child, my family was sitting at the dinner table when my dad casually announced to my mom that a longtime associate was leaving the bank. He explained that she had been recruited by another financial institution that was offering considerably more money for her to make the switch. She had decided it was an offer she could not refuse, and my father was clearly sad to see her go.

Mom had known this woman since she was a part-time clerk at the bank—she'd actually started work at Third Federal in high school. This woman was integral to Third Federal, one of the associates who understood the mission of the bank and the unique connection we have to our customers. My mother wasn't having it.

Mom stood up from the table, rising to her full five-foot height, and firmly told my father that he was absolutely not to let this associate go, as she was too valuable to Third Federal and to him. She insisted that he needed to do whatever it took to get her to stay.

As he often did, Dad listened to Mom, and the next day he offered that associate a considerable raise to stay with Third Federal. My mom's passion was well placed because that associate worked another twenty years for Dad, eventually rising to head of our Escrow division. To top it off, she then spent another twenty-six years working with me, ultimately retiring as a senior-level associate overseeing retail operations in Ohio, where most of our associates work. She did all of this with a high school education. What a great example of what people can achieve at Third Federal! This is one of the many instances that showed that my mother knew what she was talking about.

Even more than this, however, this episode, just one among many, showed the importance of respect, another of Third Federal's values. Mom and Dad always respected each other. My mother respected the associate in question enough to highly value her. My father respected both my mother and the associate enough to offer a raise. The associate respected us enough to tell us about her plans and give us a chance to keep her on board. Without respect, any one of these steps might have fallen apart and led to a very different outcome for all of us. Heck, my siblings and I respected my parents enough to listen in on them as they discussed what, to a child, might seem like mundane business dealings. We all shared a mutual respect, and we all benefited from it.

Respect is critical. It's why it's one of the values at Third Federal. It has these apparent benefits that many people could trace, but it often leads to even more intangible benefits. Clearly, I respect my mom as an insightful counselor, a dedicated and supportive mother, and also a skilled businesswoman. What became apparent to me over time is that this respect, and seeing such respect from my father, made it so that it was no big thing to assume that other women could be integral to the success of Third Federal. I grew up with a healthy respect for women, knowing that, just like my mom, they were just as capable as men. This also, naturally, extends to many of the other traits that society tends to use to marginalize or segment itself—race, gender, age, income level, religion. My upbringing and the example of my parents helped me to realize how erroneous it is to walk into an interaction with preconception about someone's capability based on their identity.

My respect for women in the workplace has been a huge advantage for me as the leader of Third Federal. We don't have preconceptions about gender roles and work performance. This goes for men or women; we are simply looking for the best associate, and it has led us to have a variety of viewpoints, skill sets, and ideas at Third Federal. It's made it so that a large variety of perspectives have influenced our decisions, both major and minor.

At various times, the Third Federal workforce has been upward of 80 percent women. For much of our recent history, 50 percent of my direct reports have been women. We have equal hiring practices, pay schedules, and promotion criteria for women and men. There has been a long history of respect for the women working at Third Federal, where we are proud to say that there is no glass ceiling.

Allowing people to earn respect without being dismissed by preconceptions has allowed Third Federal to become what it is today.

That respect extends between our associates, to their families, and to all our customers. Our organization, products, and work culture reflect this, and it's one of our greatest assets.

Teamwork Is Based on Respect

So how does an organization create an atmosphere that fosters respect? One of the things we do is to emphasize the achievements of teams and groups rather than heaping glory upon an individual leader. We want to make sure that everyone in the bank is aware that we know of their contributions and that we know how critical they are—even if those accomplishments aren't necessarily as visible as those of their colleagues. We want everyone in the company to be aware of these ideas—to that end, we frequently make an effort to bolster and reinforce that teamwork with special events and visiting public figures.

One of these special events that sticks out in my memory is a speaking engagement Third Federal had with athlete Brandi Chastain. She was one of the star players who helped the US Women's National Team become the World Soccer Champions in 1999. Her list of accomplishments, including two Olympic gold medals, was extensive. She wasn't an underachiever; her accomplishments were substantial by any measure. Despite this, the talk she delivered to our associates wasn't about these lofty achievements. She, instead, had a core theme that she returned to again and again—that all of her accomplishments came about not just because of her individual skill but also because of the mutual respect she, her teammates, and her coaches had for each other. The players trusted the coaches to create plays and respond to the strategy of a game. They trusted the supply managers and trainers. They trusted their teammates to complete the plays as they were written and to respond as needed when things changed. This trust existed because they respected one another—they knew their teammates had the ability and know how to do what's best.

Chastain said that athletic goals are only partly about scores and times. They're equally about relationships of trust and respect among players, parents, coaches, and fans. She said that no matter how well an individual athlete performs, a team made up of players who have built up respect for each other will achieve more. As Chastain noted, a relay team will almost always beat a single athlete's time. Once the distance gets long enough, no single athlete can carry the baton all the way to the finish line at a full sprint.

As a lifelong sports fan, I often paraphrase what Tom Brady said when he was asked to analyze the success he has had playing for Bill Belichick—"He was there to coach football, I was there to play football."[24] The simplicity of such a statement hides a lot of depth. As much of a star as Brady was, like Chastain, he realized that success is about more than where the attention goes. Seeing these attitudes in action in people with such great achievements truly underlines how important these ideas are.

Sometimes fostering respect in your company might take some big leaps and some significant guidelines. For instance, for most of our history, Third Federal generally has not allowed associates to work from home, and since the pandemic, we offer hybrid schedules rather than fully remote positions. Emailing and video conferencing from home may have their advantages, but in other ways, they undermine the effort to reinforce a culture of caring. At Third Federal, we believe that our associates will be at their best if they are able to get to know each other and work closely. If we don't see each other, we'll never know each other. If we don't know each other, we really can't implement our values in the way that our company culture demands.

---

24   *Man in the Arena: Tom Brady*, Episode 9 ESPN+, 2021.

In other companies, it is not uncommon for a worker to never see fellow employees, or their boss, in person.

Third Federal isn't alone in this approach. I recall that the first big—and perhaps now infamous—thing former Yahoo CEO Marissa Mayer instituted when she took over at the company, was a policy that required remote workers to start coming to the office. She was widely criticized for this change, as many employees had joined Yahoo based on the ability to work remotely. Despite these objections, it's hard to disagree with her fundamental desire to have people collaborate in physical proximity to each other because that generates an environment of closeness and respect that you can't replicate with a remote staff. And being in the same office is the first step to collaboration and creativity.

This, of course, presented some challenges during the COVID-19 pandemic, but our culture of respect enabled us to move past that. After we issued laptops, we worked with our cameras on, in close contact, and with constant communication. We made sure that we conducted ourselves as if we were in person. To top that off, we made modifications to our offices so that we could work in person as soon as it was safe to do so. We thrive as a community, and we did our best to keep the pandemic from slowing that down. We were able to transition to remote work with remarkable ease, a fact that I ascribe to our culture of mutual respect and caring.

There are corporate cultures where you don't sit at the head of any meeting room table. "That's where the boss sits," you're told, and anyone else sitting there would be viewed as being disrespectful and presumptuous. It doesn't seem unreasonable considering the consciousness of that culture. It separates associates into leaders and followers, and that's often what shortsighted organizations want.

Whether it's in person or via video conference, at Third Federal, we try to perpetuate an attitude that emphasizes that we are in this together and that we can rely on that togetherness because of our mutual respect. We want this to be reflected in our corporate culture, so, where we could, we installed round tables in our headquarters' common areas, lunch rooms, and conference rooms. The roundness of our tables emphasizes that everyone's ideas and opinions are respected and given equal consideration. The concept is so important to us that we even designed our headquarters so that the central feature is a rotunda.

All these changes arose out of my early drive to shift the culture of Third Federal so that we could work in ways t hat would bring in a bigger variety of viewpoints and experiences. I knew that our organization would really benefit from this expansion of thought, and my early experiences really emphasized this.

Call Me Marc

My early tenure at Third Federal was characterized by trying to implement the values everyone else just gave lip service to. This included the value of respect. Even though it was always a polite place, Third Federal definitely changed for the better when respect became a matter of principle, not just a point of decorum. During my dad's time, he would walk through the 7007 Broadway Avenue headquarters and resounding down the halls would be the many greetings to "Mr. Stefanski." Use of surnames was expected.

Dad formed teams to undertake projects. I had been assigned to lead a team that made some early and awkward attempts to incorporate computers into the operation because even Dad, who liked stability and tradition, could see the handwriting on the wall: pencil and paper were on their way out.

The initial steps toward modernization on the computer front was a bit slow at first. We were inputting loan information from paper and entering it into a database, and it needed to change. I asked an entry-level associate to join us. She already knew how to encode loan information digitally, so she was the perfect choice despite her freshman status. After she joined us, we finally made real progress. Within that early computer technology team, respect was conveyed personally, rank was unimportant, and success was achieved by learning from others. Those sorts of small moments help us to mature. We learn that the key to success is to value a sense of belonging, a sense of accountability, and a sense of equality.

Dad's reputation for honesty and integrity was what enabled him to collect that initial $50,000 to start Third Federal. The initial investors in Third Federal respected my father and his commitment to creating a bank that was strong, stable, and safe. And he respected them enough to always make good on this commitment. Much of the growth we have achieved through the years has come from the respect we've earned and the respect we've given. This respect our community has for the people who make up Third Federal is still strong today, from the associates in our branches, to the board of directors. My father, like many in his era, mostly believed respect came as a matter of rank and status. Although he respected all his associates, he didn't necessarily have a mission to foster a sense of belonging and equality.

When my father ran the bank, he employed a command-and-control style of leadership—he was in command. He was in control. Most of my father's attention was on the health of the bank, and he generally didn't see the benefit of how the social aspects of running a business could help with relationship building and therefore help build respect. This wasn't often a hindrance for him, but it's hard to know how things might have been different if he'd approached the corporate culture of Third Federal from a different, respect-based perspective. My father was very cost-conscious, as a bank founder should be. His primary drive was stability, probably owing to his experiences in the Great Depression. This was the right plan for his era, and I'm happy he left me with such a lasting legacy.

Third Federal needed to build on this strength by emphasizing how important interpersonal relationships are. By default, because of the corporate culture at the time, at Third Federal, respect went one direction: toward a traditional hierarchy. That focused dedication allowed me to take over a very strong bank that was primed for growth. I inherited a well-built machine, and I wanted to use that stability of Third Federal as a foundation to build a new business culture.

The first big change I made was that all Third Federal associates were expected to call each other by their respective first names. This sort of social environment makes it so that addressing another associate isn't immediately a reminder of hierarchy and rank. This was a symbolic first step, and it immediately made a difference, but there was plenty of improvement needed to take Third Federal into the new millennium besides addressing each other by our first names.

I felt that I needed to make changes and put some thought into our need to implement some well-defined personnel policies and hiring protocols. Even so, I thought the best way I could move the bank forward was to make our associates relationship managers first, and administrators and finance managers second. It would be a switch from what they had been accustomed to under my dad's leadership, but I knew that it was ultimately in the best interest of Third Federal. An organization that knows its purpose always has a distinct goal to work toward. Third Federal's purpose is upholding its five core values. We create a mutual respect with our customers and associates by adhering to these values with all our actions.

The basis for creating this new momentum was to have managers passionately engage with our values, like respect for others. I wanted them to speak as often as possible about how relationships are Third Federal's first priority, which was to be then followed by financial metrics. Initially, this effort felt awkward, like trying to kick a soccer ball with your nondominant foot. The early years of trying to enact our values taught me that creating and discussing values are easier than institutionalizing them. After quite a bit of patience, practice, and perseverance on the part of our associates, we were able to incorporate our values into the language of our culture.

The change in Third Federal from the time I took over to the present day has been a big one. As I previously mentioned, we dropped the term "employee" because of the connotation the repeated use of that term comes to signify—that there is a caste system based around payroll. It implies that there were levels of respect: one level for important people and a different level for the rank and file who are merely "employed." We replaced "employee" with "associate" in a conscious effort to unify the respect all associates deserve. Being an associate de-emphasizes the transactional nature of a business and instead emphasizes the community Third Federal represents. To help reinforce the change in language in the very beginning of the program, we had fun with it: if anyone said the "E" word (employee), they had to pay a dollar to charity, or do ten push-ups.

The atmosphere of mutual respect I wanted to foster really began to flourish when we reinforced our culture in these ways to make it a part of our day-to-day.

Respect Is an Economic Decision

Hiring is expensive; firing is ridiculously expensive. It's a much better investment to keep associates happy and productive. In our eight-five-year history, Third Federal has never laid off an associate in a cost-cutting measure. We've been able to retain associates at a much higher rate than comparable banks largely due to how dynamic our associates are. As we developed our team system, we learned that we could get creative about how to put people into the right jobs in the right way.

We first learned this from our efforts to staff for the seasonal variations in our industry. Traditionally, the spring through the fall are the big months for mortgages. During those months we would reinforce the staff at the Third Federal headquarters mortgage department with qualified associates from branches around Northeast Ohio rather than bringing on any seasonal help. This also allowed us to test out "mixing and matching" our associates. During this period, wearing name tags was a must because these associates were in strange new places away from their home branches. Name tags make a business setting more personal—they also help me because I'm, frankly, bad with names. Because of the company-wide values of trust and respect, even these associates who didn't necessarily know one another in a personal capacity knew that they were working with capable, devoted, fellow professionals from Third Federal. Our associates demonstrated that they could hit the ground running and organize complex endeavors. The seasonal overstaffing seemed to go better and better as our core values became more manifest in our culture.

Many of our projects are undertaken by teams based on what we learned from staffing the seasonal rush on mortgages. Selecting team members is based upon demonstrated skill, not on rank. Teams are formed of associates who know their stuff, who want to do the work, and who are directed by managers who are not trying to protect their turf. We also want our associates to experience working with as many other associates as possible. When the job is done, the team disbands, but not before having the chance to learn about each other, grow our team dynamic, and see how our skills combine. This system, ultimately, builds up an immense amount of respect among our associates, and it makes Third Federal an incredibly flexible organization.

Not surprisingly, hiring the right sort of person who will become a successful Third Federal associate is of the utmost importance to us. Because we don't want anyone to fail, we're careful to hire talented people who will subscribe to our values, even when that means we might have to engage in additional training for our new hires. We look for competencies and values over individual, teachable skills. Skills can be taught; values often run deeper and take longer to impart if they don't come naturally.

Like any bank, we get our share of applicants who think respect comes from having a private office, a personal secretary, a nameplate on their door, and sole credit for their work. Some banks look to hire that sort of person, but we know that they aren't going to fit in at Third Federal. In my mind, nothing matches the satisfaction of hiring or promoting someone who is happy working within the Third Federal culture—when we're able to do so, we know we've found someone who values purpose as much as they value profit. They understand our commitment to each other, our customers, and our shareholders.

There are rough spots in maintaining this philosophy because bureaucracy is hard to keep suppressed. Companies have a tendency toward becoming institutions, and institutions foster bureaucracy. You want to see a company or entity in trouble? It's one that indulges red tape, bureaucracy, and internal politics. To that end, a company needs to make every effort to get out of its own way even as it's implementing cultural change.

Making Company Culture
an Asset, Not a Liability

As you implement changes in your company culture, it's critical to make sure that you don't overemphasize any of your values. For instance, around 2004, I heard that our associates were no longer scheduling same-day appointments with our customers, which I found extremely distressing. I found this out during a meeting where we were discussing how we implemented our company values. The associates were actually proud to tell me since they thought it was such an equitable decision. The managers in question weren't doing this as a form of goldbricking or laziness—in reality, they'd begun to enact this approach *because* of our core value of respect. They wanted to respect the time and schedule of the loan officers and customer service reps and ensure that they weren't overrun. They didn't want the customers to deal with a longer-than-usual wait or processing time, either—so their solution, out of respect, was to turn the customer away and to ask them to return at a later date.

"What?" I thought. "Turn a customer away for a later date? You've got to be kidding me."

It turned out that these branches weren't just scheduling appointments for the next day but often even beyond that. This, of course, goes against any sales or service technique because once a customer has left, there's a good chance they'll seek service elsewhere or just not return at all. It's the kind of thing that could grievously harm a business if it becomes routine—and apparently it had at these locations.

It seemed like an out-and-out foul-up, but as I talked to our associates and found out more about their motivation, I learned that there was more to it. They were, in a way, addressing some systemic slowdowns with the tools they had available. This, ultimately, was an attempt to be respectful to one's fellow associates, but it failed to take into account respect for the customer—we needed to be mindful of their time and to make sure our respect for them came first. This made me realize that we needed some changes to try and reduce bureaucracy, which was hindering our treating the customers with the kind of respect they deserve. Aside from the basic courtesy of it, there's the fact that if we can't serve customers where and when they need help, they'll find another bank that can.

As I investigated the matter, I began to understand the barriers they faced. That's not to say I was satisfied, but we agreed that we needed to make changes to ensure that we respected our customers' time. We needed to serve them immediately.

We built an internal campaign we called "Yes! We Can," complete with buttons and promotional material.

We reorganized ourselves so that our responses to customers would be quick and efficient. We trained our branch associates, who were on the front lines serving our customers, to respect the individual and demonstrate a commitment that said "I can help you today" rather than "Can I help you?" We made sure they had the background, information, and experience to make decisions on the spot, which benefited the customer. Meanwhile, we gave the associates in our lending support teams the information they required to assist with our branch associates' needs to respond quickly to the customers sitting right in front of them.

This worked. Not only were we able to greatly speed up our service time, but we also saw our loan volume increase because customers got their questions answered on the day that they asked them. The clear respect for their time brought many of them back as return customers.

Respect for the Customer

Demonstrating the respect we have for our customers is of paramount concern to Third Federal. The "Yes! We Can" campaign was meant to emphasize this for both our associates and our customers. Customers who know that we respect their needs are more likely to choose us as their bank. I believe it's one of the many reasons we have so many multigenerational clients.

One of the ways we do this is by making sure to respect their hardearned income by keeping costs low and not leveraging profit in a way that's harmful to our customers. As I discuss in other sections, we also try to limit fee-based profits. We also avoid many of the unnecessary costs other companies incur by staying simple with our offices. We don't spend money on the luxuries other companies use to instill a fabricated sense of respect among their workforce—luxuries like big, private offices with ornate furnishings. Instead, our branches are attractive and clean, with laminate counters and photo art rather than ornate extras. We keep costs low by not only using energy-efficient lighting but also keeping many of our lights off during daylight hours. We do this even during Cleveland winters in order to save energy. I am the kind of guy who is known for walking around turning off lights where they aren't needed. All of these efforts help us in not needing to recover these costs from the pockets of our customers. This is fundamental to the core of the company.

Although we are efficient, conservative, and cost-conscious, our sole purpose is not to be a "low-cost" provider. Cutting operational costs and lowering product prices only go so far. In my experience, the record for extremely low-cost companies shows that they might be low cost for a while but that this status isn't healthy over the long term. The problem is that they're so focused on cost-containment that they lose track of the people-side of their business. Once a company sets a cost-cutting goal and achieves it, there's little reward beyond the original fanfare they might receive from management. I've seen "low-cost" companies begin to experience problems with their workers. They struggle with high rates of employee turnover and don't earn employee respect and loyalty. They often have to resort to layoffs, something I'm proud that we've never had to do. We stay modern while also keeping low costs, and this middle path makes Third Federal an exceptional bank.

Communication Is Respect

The problem we faced with delaying customer appointments was ultimately a communication issue. Solving that problem only increased the respect our associates had for one another. In *Leadership Is an Art*,[25] Max De Pree writes that respect and communication are inextricably linked. He argues that relationships inside of companies improve when information is shared in a timely, accurate way and that sharing such information inevitably leads to trust and respect. It also enables a business to be much more effective in its operations.

One of the best illustrations of the concept comes from the early career of US Army General Norman Schwarzkopf. He was tasked with preparing a division of helicopters for operations. This unit he was taking over had a deplorable record—they'd never prepared an adequate number of choppers for deployment in recent history. Shockingly, Schwarzkopf came away from the situation looking like an amazing leader. He got the unit up to snuff and provided the appropriate number of aircraft.

When he was later asked how he'd done this, his answer was simple—he'd relayed the exact orders he'd received from his superiors

---

25   Max De Pree, *Leadership Is an Art* (East Lansing: Michigan State University Press, 1987).

to those who worked below him in the command structure. No previous commander had done so, and so the personnel in the unit hadn't even known why they were falling short of the expectations of the leadership. Schwarzkopf, rather than trying to learn the ins-and-outs of aeronautical engineering, made his way through the unit structure and made sure the entire unit knew how many choppers needed to be operational and by when. Schwarzkopf didn't know a thing about helicopters, but he did know that a clearly communicated goal would be met with more effectiveness and enthusiasm than mysterious orders or unskilled interference.[26]

His respect for his fellow soldiers and the communication this fostered led his unit to flourish.

Clear communication, and the accompanying respect demonstrated for one's peers, is a tool that helps me lead successfully. When Third Federal has a strategy, I try to make it company-wide. For example, I've learned that our mission statement and our values need to be in our literature, spoken aloud at our meetings so that they are made constant points of contemplation. This communicates our goals on a company-wide level, and it demonstrates that we respect our associates enough to carry these goals to the finish line.

It's a Team Effort

Living as a garage band hero is where I hang my hat. So it's a big stretch for me to imagine being a rock star leader, the celebrity CEO. Who needs that level of attention? Who needs individual acclaim for running a business when anyone who is being honest, and thinking critically, knows that any endeavor in a business is a group effort? There is no person on this earth who can claim to be solely responsible

---

26   Norman Schwarzkopf and Peter Petre, *It Doesn't Take a Hero* (New York: Bantam Books, 1992).

for the accomplishments of their well-run business. Nevertheless, this sort of person exists. There are leaders who seek to make themselves the center of their business and thereby make the business an exercise in narcissism rather than a community endeavor.

In *Good to Great*, author Jim Collins notes that poor leadership is driven by an ambition that is first and foremost self-centered—even to the detriment of the company as a whole. A poor leader wants individual recognition for endeavors that were truly a team effort. In my opinion, this leader's drive for fame is a result of our modern culture's belief that this sort of leadership is required in order for a company to be successful. The "business as a cult of personality" has often been a feature of American business (just consider Ford and Edison), but social media and modern media coverage seem to have made this even more prolific in our era. One of my great desires is to keep Third Federal from ever falling into such a pattern.

This doesn't mean that ambition itself is a problem. Ambition is, after all, necessary for any endeavor to have any vision or growth. Collins points out that ambition should be "first and foremost for the cause, for the organization and its purpose."[27] Successful leadership often comes from a place of humility. Similarly, the success of a business leader has little to do with having an outgoing, type A personality. Collins writes that great leadership comes down to the presence of a "Level 5" leader, which he describes as follows:

"While Level 5 leaders can come in many personality packages, they are often self-effacing, quiet, reserved, and even shy. [They] motivate the enterprise more with inspired standards than inspiring personality."

---

27   Jim Collins, *Good to Great* (New York: Harper Collins, 2001).

We stress to our leadership that it is more important to "lead from behind" than it is to get credit. It demonstrates the respect we have for our associates and our trust that the job will get done. Our clear communication, our emphasis on the power of listening, our respect for our customers, and the fact that we're all in it together will carry the day.

Not having this respect can be the doom of an organization. I've seen the executives of other companies fall victim to their own overinflated egos. They don't respect the opinions of their colleagues, they don't communicate with their organizations, and they waste money on hollow window dressing like fancy office complexes. These are patterns I've seen preceding a bank shuttering for good, and it can be grim. This is the last thing I want for myself, let alone for Third Federal.

The associates at Third Federal have helped our leadership not only to succeed but also to get out of our own way and lean on the expertise of our peers. My unending respect for my peers at Third Federal has made our bank solid and secure, and I know that the respect we show to our associates and customers is one of the reasons that Third Federal has endured.

The Wooden Bowl— A Parable about Respect

As he neared the end of his life, an old man moved in with his son and his family. The son had great wealth as he had taken over his father's thriving business. His father had been a renowned builder.

Although he'd been powerful in his day, the old man was now bent and aged. He could barely see, and his grandchildren had to guide him to the table where the family dined.

As frail as he was, he did his best to make his family happy, singing the great old tales and poems his family loved.

His voice was beautiful, and it seemed to stay young forever.

Unfortunately, the rest of him did not. As he ate, his hands shook, knocking over cups and plates, sending food sprawling. He couldn't see or hear when he shattered the fine dishes his son had bought.

When the broken dishes and spilled food became too much, his daughter-in-law convinced her husband to have his father sit outside and eat from a wooden bowl, the one dish that wouldn't shatter when it was dropped.

The grandfather didn't complain, but his songs took on a somber tone. The family could hear him, faintly, as they ate, dining his last days away, alone in the open air.

One morning, the father came across his son, sitting with his grandfather in the courtyard, carving another wooden bowl.

"Son, you're carving a new bowl for your grandfather, how kind!"

"Oh no, father, this one is for you when you get old and must eat outside," his son replied.

The man was ashamed of what he'd taught his son and brought his father back inside.

From that day until the day he passed, the family was grateful for every song that echoed off the walls their patriarch had built.

This parable about respect captures the way we use it to be better together than we are alone. Sending the grandfather outside could be seen as the equivalent of a short-term tactic that ultimately degrades the organization. And those tactics have a cost. When the son took the time to reflect upon the nature of respect, he brought his own father back in, and the family was better for it.

> Respect enhances us, and it's something that's always worth striving toward. And, as they say, respect costs nothing but yields great returns.

Excellence

Nobody Does It Better

—CARLY SIMON

By the end of the 2008 mortgage crisis, Third Federal was still standing, and in better shape than most of the competition. This is because we hold our associates to a higher standard in terms of commitment to the job, production, dedication, and loyalty.

Let me take you into the Third Federal inner sanctum as the 2008 mortgage crisis mounted. For this story to make sense, you need to know that we are an organization that is so conservative that we think yellow sticky notes are a waste of paper. Our inclination is toward safe business practices, but during this era, our resolve was being tested by the relentless drive toward the profit-at-all-costs model that was sweeping the banking industry. This rapidly became a time when most banks considered no mortgage to be too risky. They'd lend to almost anyone under any terms, and they, at least initially, were profiting from it. In our pursuit of being top in our marketplace, we almost plunged right off the same cliff these organizations were about to plunge over as the housing market crashed due to the bad loans that they were making.

We might have been pulled into the same vortex, but our belief that we should always strive for excellence was the value that saved us from plunging down this same path. For Third Federal, excellence means excellent service to excellent customers at excellent rates. We opted to continue down the path of excellence rather than to take up risky bulk lending like other banks.

During that time, as we watched our residential mortgage market share take a dive, we weren't sure that our conservative approach to mortgage lending would hold up. If we had wavered in the way we do business, who knows where we'd be today. In Cuyahoga County, which is our long-standing area of influence in Ohio, our market share for residential mortgages—single-family, owner-occupied homes— had historically hovered in the 20 percent range.

But as the country's banking industry went bananas with no-interest loans, "liar loans," and pick-your-payment loans, we saw that market share dip to a mere 9 percent. Companies were lending at 100 percent value on properties, even for properties with vastly inflated property value. As the bubble continued to grow, the numbers got bigger and bigger, and companies were seeing some serious profit.

This trend stunned me. Mortgages were, and are, our flagship product, and we were losing out in our home market. We began to worry that we were not upholding our commitment to excellence by missing out on an opportunity for growth and reinvestment. The market was in a feeding frenzy. I worried that we were failing our stakeholders by not being there to fulfill that demand.

The management team at Third Federal had not engaged in any of the behaviors that were causing the market to boom. I called them into a meeting and challenged them, saying, "Why shouldn't we make interest-only, low-doc or pick-your-payment loans to lower-quality customers? Everyone else is!"

We made the right decision in the end, but now, looking back, I'm a little surprised, and perhaps mildly embarrassed, that it wasn't immediately obvious to me that we shouldn't be making these sorts of loans. It wasn't the right thing to do, and the nature of them ultimately violates our core values of trust and love. At the time, however, the outcome of the mortgage crash wasn't a known factor, and our competitors were offering them. I was busy watching them profit from the current-day realities of the market while we did not. It would be enough to tempt any entrepreneur.

The shift in the mortgage market was nationwide, and there was a similar dynamic going on in Florida, where we were trying to gain market share as quickly as possible. Despite this drive to expand, we were intent on only making loans for homes that someone intended to live in as their primary residence. This kept us out of the speculation market and kept us from suffering when it fell.

Just like in Ohio, this was different from the behavior of our competition in Florida. Other Florida banks were making investment property home loans to investors who intended to make a tidy profit by flipping them to other buyers. Frequently, in the Florida market, our competitors were giving mortgages to individuals who generally had no business having more than one property but who often, in fact, had five or more properties that they intended to sell off at a great profit. These were speculative investments that the buyers couldn't afford. This fact, however, didn't stop our competitors in Florida, and across the country, from approving buyers who couldn't make a down payment and who couldn't pay down principal. These borrowers only paid the interest, and when the value of the house decreased, they couldn't sell it, and the property turned into an investment loss. This often meant that the borrower in question would slide into insolvency and bankruptcy.

We always strive toward being strong, stable, and safe. That kind of stability builds and sustains relationships and focuses on caring for our customers. Despite this tradition, as we watched this market rush, we felt like we saw that threat of Third Federal potentially fading into irrelevance. Like many other institutions, we were at a crossroads, and it was uncertain that we'd take the right path.

That's when our management team stepped up. They considered Third Federal's mission statement even as I was almost blinded by the potential of the rapidly changing market. Our mission statement was what ultimately became the beacon that kept us on track: "We help families achieve the dream of home ownership and financial security. We create value for our customers, our communities, our associates and our shareholders." It is a mission with a moral compass that goes all the way back to my dad's belief that perpetuating sound lending practices was the single-most important thing a savings and loan could do.

The management team forecast what would happen if Third Federal made no-doc, low-doc, interest-only loans with no down payment or subpar underwriting to those who could not afford them. It was the same thing that would happen if we made investor property loans to lower credit quality customers—eventually, interest rates would rise or housing values would plummet, and these loans would never be paid back. It became obvious that there were actually numerous economic scenarios where these hypothetical customers wouldn't be able to repay their loans. We couldn't sustainably offer all these types of mortgages because the math behind these loans didn't work for us. That's because the math didn't work for our customers. As it turns out, the math didn't work for anyone who wasn't willing to tank the market just to make a profit.

In my heart, I understood that the long-term, subprime loans were not aligned with our mission of secure home ownership, nor were they in line with our history of being strong, stable, and safe.

Cranking up the number of transactions with subprime loans would have looked good on paper. We'd have shown more activity, and even with our minimal fee structure, we'd make money, but it wouldn't have lived up to our core vision of successful home ownership for our customers.

After reviewing all our options, our management team finally recommended that Third Federal not enter the subprime market because we would be offering home ownership without financial security. Our customers relied on our expertise to get them into safe products. Helping them buy a home they would likely lose would violate our commitment to excellence, they said. It would be unethical and would wreck our integrity as a bank.

Shortly after we made this decision, the financial market caved in.

And it was now clear that the lost market share we endured in this time had been worth it. We have always strived to be a leader in market share in each of our markets, and none of us were pleased about losing market share, but we *were* pleased that staying out of the subprime market fray kept us true to our commitment to excellence.

Entering the subprime lending market would have been disastrous for Third Federal. When the mortgage crisis hit, our low exposure to subprime loans became the key to our survival even as other banks folded under the weight of their failed subprime portfolios.

As huge banks and thrifts had to be rescued by the government or taken over by the Federal Deposit Insurance Corporation (FDIC), we were OK. Still, even some of our very solid borrowers were forced to default despite our best efforts to help them. Despite this, the five-star rating we had been given by Bauer Financial, Inc., an independent agency that rates banks based on soundness, stayed with us. In fact, we've had our five-star rating for more than thirty-five years, and it is still ours today.

A Diamond in the Rough

Amid the devastating bank failures during the mortgage crisis, Third Federal managed to elevate its performance despite the catastrophic market. The capital ratio of a bank is a measure of the proportion of capital the bank has relative to its assets. This ratio is critical because it is a measure of how stable the bank is. Having more capital protects a bank from the risk of assets losing their value. Third Federal currently has a tier-one capital ratio around 10 percent. When the mortgage crisis hit, regulators increased the capital requirements and required banks to risk weight their assets, increasing the required capital ratio minimums by 50 percent. At that time, our ratio was over 15 percent, more than two times the requirement to be considered well capitalized.

As a result of our initial public offering (IPO) in 2007, Third Federal had grown by about $1 billion. The new cash infused into our company bolstered our capital ratio to 17 percent, which many investors had told us was too high. They'd insisted that the cash would be better utilized if we were to use it to expand into new markets and/or buy back shares of stock, so much so that it would force us to go fully public. Nevertheless, we managed our capital carefully and deployed it with discipline and purpose. That approach was more in line with our values. The extra $1 billion provided by our IPO saved us an immense amount of trouble. While our investors didn't understand the strength that capital provides in taking care of the company, associates, customers, and communities, we did.

Here's what outside analysts often don't understand about Third Federal—that my father's experience in the Great Depression still guides the bank to this day. My father always made sure the bank had more than enough capital. My father also only found new markets in clients who he knew would pay back their loans. He was not only flexible but also careful. Third Federal invests heavily in its community, but the risks we take are very calculated. When we give loans in less-than-ideal circumstances, we make sure they are endeavors that are going to improve the communities we serve.

To reinforce this and provide stability, we stay profitable by focusing our marketing strategies on attracting strong customers who will pay us back. This strategy has helped us to keep a capital ratio that is well above that of our competitors. All of this means that, as much as we would like to help them, borrowers who intend to engage in speculation or flipping are welcome to look elsewhere. That conservative approach is the right thing to do for Third Federal, and it is the basis for our commitment to excellence. Simultaneously, Third Federal has a large commitment to lending in its communities, ensuring that we provide growth that helps everyone thrive.

We don't get people into homes just to take them away again later, which is exactly what would have happened had we gotten caught up in the subprime craze. Our other values of love, trust, and respect for our customers would have been thrown by the wayside had we done so. Over the years, I've noticed that the guiding stars of our institutional values lead us to excellence again and again.

"Perfect Is the Enemy of the Good"

A commitment to excellence involves constant evaluation. Are you setting the bar high enough? Are you engaging with the needs of both associates and customers? Are you constantly questioning your own perspective? Are you adhering to your values while you do all this?

The associates at Third Federal are trained to ask themselves the following: What kind of quality and diligence are we putting into our relationships? Are we fully satisfied with the way we help our customers? If not, is there room for improvement in those interactions and tasks?

We should reach toward excellence but only with the purpose of illuminating our own path—not with the purpose of perfection. It is easy to allow the desire to be excellent to become tyrannical if we don't think of it in the right way. While it's great to be excellent, we should not demand perfection from ourselves.

A true drive for excellence involves a number of endeavors where perfectionism is virtually impossible. People who strive for excellence have a strong need for order and organization, but they also need to understand that not all will be ordered. Reacting to chaos, and sometimes even creating it, is a part of growth and innovation. Those who strive toward excellence obviously have high expectations for themselves, but they also need to be able to accept their own mistakes and have positive ways of coping with those situations where perfection is impossible. One of the most vital traits of a person who achieves excellence is that they are able to both recognize and learn from their mistakes.

Excellence doesn't have to be perfect. Author Gordon Livingston wrote that "perfect is the enemy of the good."[28] His thought, which has also been attributed to Confucius, is that demanding perfection paralyzes us. Perfection is not a real thing. It's ultimately unobtainable, and the belief that we've achieved it might even keep us from addressing our errors and learning from them. Mistakes can be opportunities. They offer a chance to change and reevaluate. As counterintuitive as it seems, experience has shown me that many people think more highly of Third Federal after we've made a mistake and addressed it. Correcting a mistake gives any institution a chance to show its customers that it really cares about their experience and their results. Circling back

---

28   Gordon Livingston, *Too Soon Old, Too Late Smart: Thirty True Things You Need to Know Now* (Boston, MA: Da Capo Press; Perseus Books, 2004).

and fixing a mistake also underlines the institution's commitment to its values—for both it's customers and associates.

Third Federal almost engaging with the subprime mortgage market, for instance, was an opportunity for learning. A perfectionist might just sweep such a moment under the rug. I believe excellence is about engaging with such potential mistakes.

Although there are many specific instances of Third Federal associates doing a great job of doing their best to correct mistakes and make sure the customer experience is excellent, an anecdote involving one of our long-term customers comes to mind.

I received a complaint letter from a customer after he'd visited Third Federal to apply for a mortgage. His application was eventually turned down, but that wasn't the thing that had upset him. What upset him was that he'd felt as if he had received the "run around" before he was turned away.

This customer wrote to me directly and told me that he'd been left feeling like we did not care about his experience. He went on to explain that he'd expected his mortgage application might be rejected, but that he'd come in anyway because he trusted Third Federal, and he'd wanted to discuss possible alternative scenarios and to have us help him weigh his options. After all, he and his family had relied on Third Federal for decades. Instead of receiving the excellent care he'd come to expect, he felt that he'd been met with needless delays and a perfunctory dismissal when the loan wasn't approved.

Even though we couldn't give him the loan, I didn't like that we'd let him down or made him feel dismissed. His family had a long-term deposit in our bank, he owned stock from our IPO, and he'd been a customer at Third Federal for fifty years. This wasn't someone the bank should disappoint—let alone lose.

The morning after I'd received his letter, I made sure he was contacted by Third Federal associates, who addressed his feelings of mistreatment and discussed his mortgage options with him. After everything was settled, he contacted me again. He told me that he appreciated it and that the quick response and the individual attention were exactly why he and his family have been a part of Third Federal for a half century.

All in all, things ended well, but the experience contains an important lesson about excellence. We don't need to be perfect the first time. Or ever. We just need to always strive toward excellence.

This experience let us keep a customer who, disappointed by the rejection, might have ended up at a different bank. Our effort to make things right was impressive enough that he's still a customer a decade later.

This customer's story and stories like his have impacted the way we handle processing mortgage applications and other banking matters. We've learned from past mistakes. We ensure that the customers get time to discuss their circumstances, to plan alternatives, and to tell us about anything else we need to know. It's probably something efficiency experts would abhor, but it's a practice that lets us build the kinds of trust and respect that allow us to keep customers even after we've made mistakes. It lets them know that even when things go wrong, we care, and we'll address them. Even more than that, our ability to strive for excellence while ignoring the false promise of perfection has let us continue to evolve and change.

Most would say it's better to get it right that first time. This is especially true of the leaders who organize their business only around efficiency and hard metrics. The metric of this individual customer, in the grand scheme of things, wouldn't have had much impact on Third Federal as a whole. But not addressing this mistake once ensures it'll happen over and over.

There's a Zen parable that captures how achievement can be confused as the point of an endeavor rather than a by-product.

Our Moon

One night long ago, a nun and a Zen master were tending to a garden, digging up and pulling weeds under the full moon. The nun had resolved that tonight she would approach the Zen master for help with some particularly elusive concepts. She admired his gift for understanding doctrine and his ability to grapple with difficult ideas. As they finished their work and prepared to turn in for the evening, she reached out and touched his shoulder.

She said to him, "I've been studying the Nirvana Sutra for years and years, but there are still some passages I don't quite understand. Can you help me with this passage?"

She produced a carefully rolled sheet of paper from her robes and unfurled it, holding the note-covered page out for the monk's examination.

He stared at the page for a few moments, brushing his fingers across the ink, and then shook his head with a faint smile.

"I'm sorry," he said, "but I can't read. If you can read the passages out for me, I'll see if I can help you understand them."

The nun's brow furrowed; she tried to hide her surprise.

"Forgive me, sir, if you can't even read the words, how can you understand the truth behind them?"

She could see his smile widen, half-hidden by the shadows of a fruit tree. He stepped fully into the silver light and pointed up at the moon overhead.

> *"The truth and the words are unrelated. The truth can be compared to the moon. And words can be compared to a finger. I can use my finger to point out the moon, but my finger is not the moon."*
>
> *The moon was huge and distant, dwarfing both of them.*
>
> *"You don't need my finger to see the moon, do you?"*
>
> *The nun did not.*[29]

The metrics traditional business leaders often use to measure excellence don't really engender trust, respect, or love—and they, therefore, can't lead to the kind of reliable excellence that has kept Third Federal thriving over the years.

More often than not, our values ensure that our first interaction with a customer *will* be excellent. That's because rather than merely working just for a paycheck, Third Federal associates are truly invested in supporting its values as their own—especially when interacting with customers. As commonly understood, "volunteers" make a personal commitment to a meaningful cause.

For Third Federal to be successful, each associate must fully invest into our objective of using our core values in all their interactions with our key stakeholders—fellow associates, our customers, and our various communities. We operationalize this priority institution-wide by the way in which we hire and evaluate our associates. When our associates are reviewed, we don't measure them based on fulfilling quotas. We, instead, look at their interactions using our values with the key groups and associates they interact with. We reinforce that these values are the core of what we do. We de-emphasize the

---

29   Adapted from Arthur Sokoloff, *Life without Stress: The Far Eastern Antidote to Tension and Anxiety* (New York: Broadway Books, 1997).

numbers, which is part of our strategy on not paying commission. Instead, we offer stability by providing a long, steady career for the associates who engage with our values. An associate finds success at Third Federal by engaging in our cultural concepts of trust, love, respect, excellence, and fun.

We're also committed to letting someone move on if they aren't a good fit for our values. Avoiding the pitfalls of perfectionism doesn't mean that we engage in the sunk cost fallacy and pour time and effort into people and scenarios that won't work out.

As a final, practical look at the matter, I present a quote from General Patton, who was famous for saying "[a] good plan, violently executed now, is better than a perfect plan next week."[30] This is as true of banking as it must be for war. We're in a marketplace full of fierce competition. Speed to market is extremely important, and you sometimes need to "commit to committing," and be aware that you'll need to navigate any difficulties you encounter along the way.

If you wait for perfection, you'll never get out of the gate.

Excellence Everywhere

While constructing the Third Federal campus-style headquarters on Broadway Avenue in Cleveland and succeeding with our Ohio expansion in the late 1990s, we explored expanding Third Federal into Florida. The key to deciding to go ahead with our expansion was based on having a reputation for excellence.

Third Federal maintains a high level of excellence by embracing the fact that we need to be responsive and adaptive even as we engage in rigorous planning and strategy. While we prefer often to take a conservative approach to our businesses, our values have made us

---

30 George Patton Jr., *The War as I Knew it* (Boston, MA: Houghton Mifflin Company, 1947).

flexible and cohesive enough that we can make quick decisions and be intuitive and nimble whenever needed.

Third Federal did quite a bit of planning and research before we expanded out of state. We also, however, made our decision on where to expand based on where our customers were going during the winter months or when they moved away for their retirement.

When we looked at expanding into Florida, we spent a considerable amount of time analyzing potential branch locations once we had a broad overview of where many ex-Ohioans were located. We used computer listings to further narrow our focus to where Clevelanders were located and drew on whatever other resources we could use to pinpoint individual neighborhoods that would serve as strong market locations, and then we let commercial real estate experts guide us in selecting our final branch locations.

We kept track of our customers who had large savings accounts. Over the decades, we would contact them when their CDs were getting close to their maturity dates, and we found that these customers had often relocated to Florida in their retirement. We began our expansion there knowing we would have existing customers to build upon.

Florida was over-banked at the turn of the millennium, but none of the banks in the existing market were offering what Third Federal offered: low mortgage rates, high savings rates, and great customer service. These are all things a good bank is meant to offer, of course, and any other bank could have done it, but none did. By the late 1990s, many small, community banks in Florida had been sold to large, out-of-state commercial banks. We knew Floridians were not altogether happy about this depersonalization, so we saw an opportunity. Leading up to our expansion, many customers had asked us, "Why don't you open Third Federal branches in Florida? We need your sort of values here."

I was confident that if we stayed fiscally conservative, we could take our philosophy and values with us to Florida, and those would lead us to the same success we had for our expansion throughout Ohio. Our early expansions were the base of our expansion across the country. We're now lending in twenty-seven states because of these practices.

In recent years, things have changed drastically in the banking industry. Third Federal has seen a shift in how most customers interact with our thrift. More than 60 percent of our loan applications now come in from the internet. We've remained successful in this new arena by keeping the same values we have for in-person customers. Rates are locked in at the time of the application; the process is transparent and doesn't involve excessive questions. We realize that not everyone wants to deal with a loan officer, but we also make them available if they're needed. Our process won't drag individuals who can't be approved through unnecessary steps, and it approves those it can as quickly as possible.

In many ways, our online presence has become our biggest branch. We have a cutting-edge front end and an easily accessible service branch. We've centralized our operations across the country into a Customer Care center that's focused entirely on guiding customers through the online loan processing experience.

The continual growth we've experienced from our digital presence has been so dramatic that it continues to startle me when I think back on the fact that this technology hasn't really existed for all that long in comparison to the much longer history of Third Federal as a thrift.

Embracing new technology while holding on to our values has kept Third Federal fast, efficient, and friendly—we're quick to respond to problems and we care. We make sure you can reach a human being, and we know that there will always be customers who want to physically come to the bank in person.

Don't Get in Your Own Way

We were confident of our eventual success in new markets because of the expectation that our commitment to excellence would translate there— excellence is, after all, universal. We just tried to not trip over ourselves.

The Leader in Me, a book by the great Stephen Covey, is targeted at youth, but one thing in its pages has always resonated with me because of how it relates to our central value of excellence: "More often than not, great initiatives are not sustainable due to systems and processes not being in place to sustain excellence."[31]

One of the other keys to excellence at Third Federal is trying to minimize unneeded bureaucratic hurdles from our work. Bureaucracies are often the systems that block our success if they are not properly set up or if they delay communication among people. We encourage associates to communicate with each other directly, to call other offices directly, and to engage in making their own decisions whenever possible. It's part of their training and also part of their evaluations.

During our expansion, it took some effort to prevent our internal processes from thwarting our efforts to expand. This was especially true with our goal of hiring only excellent people who would fit into the Third Federal culture. Good hiring practices take time and much care, which wasn't always in sync with our timetable to expand. We had to balance short-term goals of expansion with our long-term need for hiring associates who would be committed to our values. The elements that might get in the way were the same as in any large project.

Every large project is ultimately a logistics question. Do you have enough people behind the scenes working on it? Do you have the wherewithal to support it? Do you have enough money to support your initiative? How many people do you have to hire? How long will

---

31 Stephen R. Covey and Sean Covey, *The Leader in Me* (New York: Simon & Schuster, 2008).

that take? Will your information technology be able to support what you're doing? And if they can't, how long will it take for the programmers to get it up to speed while they're working on twenty different things? This is as true now as it was in the 1990s—the technology changes, but the practicalities don't. There's a lot involved, and it's easy to over-plan or under-plan to the point of paralysis.

Fortunately, we made a key hire in the form of a new regional manager for our Florida expansion. We could tell immediately that she would live by all the core values Third Federal represented, and she set about getting Third Federal's expansion moving at top speed. She was a Florida native, and she had worked in the banking industry for years. She was able to find associates she absolutely knew would also fit into Third Federal's values.

It wasn't perfect, but it was good, and it stuck to our identity and our values.

That's what matters.

We grew very quickly. We came up with a high-yield checking and savings account, and within two years, we had garnered nearly $2 billion of new money in Florida. Both products were very popular with our customers in our new market. We looked at the market, settled across the street from the competition, and then outpriced them.

Our marketing mantra was, "If we have the best rates around and the best services, why would borrowers go anywhere else?"

We widely promoted and advertised our interest rates, which generated high customer appeal. Within a few years, Third Federal had branches around the west coast of Florida, Palm Beach County, and Broward County where we collected $2.5 billion in deposits, placing us among the top twenty largest deposit holders in the state. We acquired customers one at a time, which is all we ever wanted because we knew we could retain them with great rates and great relationships. We knew they would tell their family and friends about Third Federal because that's the way a commitment to excellence pays off.

We're thriving in these places to this day, and I know without a doubt that this is due to the high standards we keep for our values.

Excellence Is the Long Game

I'll end my reflection on the value of excellence by discussing how much short-term or long-term thinking can influence our success. Short-term thinking can lead to a large amount of success or failure. People are often unwilling to take losses in the short term for bigger wins that come later. We leave the training wheels on our bike to avoid the skinned knee that is guaranteed to arise in the short term—which dooms us to never ride at the speeds a road bike could bring us. Similarly, we often gamble far too much on the short term because of the immediate gratification of quick profit. We take off the training wheels and hop straight on a motorcycle. We're going to crash, and soon, but we might go spectacularly fast for just a bit.

I believe that short-term thinking is dominating our society and has become a barrier to building long-lasting relationships. I see it in the infatuation with the immediacy of metrics, money, fame, and self-centeredness. In business, there's a similar perpetual struggle between marketing—with its seemingly immediate goals—and operations, accounting, or technology, with their desire for process and caution. Ultimately, the market obeys neither of these worldviews, and thinking that it does can lead to disaster.

Short-term thinking can definitely get results—but those results can come for the wrong reason. They can be a fluke. Focusing on process more than results has the promise of yielding more reliable results. If I know my efforts are built on a solid foundation, I know how, why, and when I'm getting my results. I can build on that process or adjust because I know how it works. A short-term, greedy strategy that is all about "efficiency experts" or cost-cutting simply doesn't leave anything to work with in the future, and it won't improve the circumstances that made the short-term thinking necessary in the first place.

This continual improvement is called Kaizen in Japanese culture, and it's something we definitely implement at Third Federal. I think that working to achieve a personal or business goal is much more likely to yield success only when it is accompanied by a commitment to invest effort across an extended period of time. Inevitably, when the going gets tough, knowledge of how necessary long-term thinking is can reinforce our staying power.

I believe in the "Flywheel" concept espoused by Jim Collins. A series of small successes can build up into sustained power—like a mechanical flywheel. An initial push and some sustained, directed efforts make a process easier to maintain. As the flywheel gathers momentum, it becomes easier to spin. The sustained refining of a process makes it easier to carry out.[32]

It seems as if many of those people who are obsessed with quick successes have little time or desire to focus on integrity or excellence, and the resulting victims are their family members, a company's customers, or perhaps society in general. A short view of the world seems to lead to shortcuts in interpersonal relationships and sometimes to failure, strife, and poor performance.

How do we mitigate these negative consequences of individualism? By placing value on our own integrity and taking the time to build long-term, values-based relationships. In our sphere of influence, Third Federal's commitment to excellence nurtures resilience and generates the fulfillment that comes from doing excellent

32   Jim Collins, *Good to Great: Why Some Companies Make the Leap and Others Don't* (Harper Business, 2001).

things for others. Sometimes that means forgoing short-term profits, market share, or earnings per share in favor of doing our best for our customers and generating a greater, more long-term profit.

Many of my bank CEO peers went into their careers working hard but were working hard at the wrong things. They could see only margins, numbers, and performance—those things became what they believed was their commitment to excellence. Some of them have never figured out that they are actually in a service and relationship industry. Some of them never made the effort to truly know their employees or their customers. They chose to follow the money, first.

As a result, many of those bankers steered the country into the 2008 mortgage crisis after the same sort of thinking had already caused the savings and loan crisis of the 1980s. These same short-term obsessions also contributed to the Great Depression. All these terrible events stemmed from the same bad motives: greed, self-preservation, and a disregard for the customer or the integrity of process.

Conversely, Third Federal's commitment to long-term, lasting excellence is what guided our expansions into Florida. We didn't think in the short term. We had such trust in our associates' commitment to excellence that we sent seasoned associates from Northeast Ohio to spend weeks at a time working with the new hires in our Florida locations – this way the associates were able to infuse our new branches with Third Federal values and promote our culture from the outset. It seemed better than trying to change the attitudes of whole teams of people we might have inherited had we acquired the workforce of an existing bank, who were likely going to operate in the more traditional, short-term culture of big numbers and quick return on investment.

The success of our Florida venture speaks volumes about how using a committed, long-term strategy has definite rewards. It was a complex effort that was driven by our dedication to taking time and doing things the right way.

Buddhism teaches us that instant gratification is not what life is all about. It is not merely material measurement that defines success. Creating meaningful, long-lasting, personal business relationships takes time.

It is not just doing a sharp-edged job that might bring accolades and performance awards. Instead, it is striving for superior performance, having a desire to do what is best for customers, family, friends, and the community. It's tying our integrity to a commitment to excellence and watching it succeed.

As a result of this core value of excellence, the average Third Federal branch, as of 2023, had approximately $300 million in deposits, while the average branch at a competing bank had around $30–$40 million. That indicates nearly ten times the trust and success of other banks. The numbers don't lie.

"How I Want to Be Remembered"

It's very easy to get caught up in a constant pursuit of bigger numbers, letting what matters fall by the wayside. When I think about how easy it is to be swept up by short-term excellence, I often think about a story I heard about another CEO.

The CEO described how hard he worked in great detail. He belabored the fact that he spent long hours away from his family, burning the midnight oil and sometimes sleeping in the office. He stressed how his company consumed everything he did, and he supposed that the company's success came from that sacrifice. Ironically, the story ends with the CEO describing how his family meant everything to him. He said, above all else, he wanted to be remembered as a good parent when people talked about his life.

I can never quite escape the irony that this story was about workaholism and a celebration of shortcuts and profit maximization at the cost of all else. In the end, there is an admonishment of how important family is. I feel a lot of pity for this person, despite my frustration at this societal attitude that encourages shortcuts and pushes an all-consuming drive for success at all costs.

This CEO was neglecting what he said he valued for the sake of petty, temporary gains. I can't help but feel bad that he squandered so much time and effort.

Excellence isn't a zero-sum game. It doesn't have to come at the expense of one's entire life, and our core values reinforce that. Excellence as a person feeds excellence as a professional, and that's something we should never forget.

The Bundle of Sticks—A Fable about Excellence

A father had a family of sons, who were forever quarreling among themselves. Talking didn't work, so the father thought long and hard about an example that would help them understand that their continued quarrels would ultimately lead to their own misfortune.

On a day that their quarreling was more violent than usual and each of the sons was moping, he asked one of them to bring him a bundle of sticks.

One at a time, he handed the bundle to each of his sons and told them to try to break it. Though each tried his best, none was able to do so.

The father then untied the bundle and gave a single stick to each of his sons and asked them to break it. This they did very easily.

"My sons," said the father, "do you not see that if you help each other, it will be impossible for your enemies to injure you? But if you are divided among yourselves, you will be no stronger than a single stick in that bundle."

In unity is strength.

Adapted from *Aesop's Fables*

Getting caught up in constant pursuit of bigger and more isn't the only trap we fall into. Excellence is also understanding that each person brings an important piece to the process and, when the team focuses on working together, that creates excellence.

Fun

Hot Fun in the Summertime

—SLY AND THE FAMILY STONE

As ironic as it seems, fun is a serious part of Third Federal's overall strategy for success. It's the way that we manage people, our message, and our delivery of value to our customers. We take ourselves seriously, but levity is important to our culture. We approach fun as a way of keeping our culture intact, reinforcing our values, and strengthening the bonds we have with each other.

One of the main ways that we accomplish all of this is with the events we have for our associates and their families. We make fun events part of our work routine at Third Federal all year long, and we promote many company-sponsored events across April, so many that we call April "Fun Month." In addition, I host a Christmas gathering for associates in each of our regions, and a summer concert and celebration for associates and their families in both Cleveland and Florida each year.

I started playing music in the seventh grade, and now some of my best memories are of standing in front of a big crowd during a warm summer night in Cleveland, and I'm belting out the words to The Beach Boys' "Barbara Ann." Managers, associates, families, and friends are all bopping around in the dance lights. We're all there to celebrate each other and everything we've done during the year. I get to play rock star, and people are enjoying it, singing along.

Associate events are a critical part of what makes Third Federal succeed. Much of what we do with these events is to tell the stories that form our institutional culture. Both on the literal level and on the metaphorical level, these gatherings give people a chance to be part of the larger community of Third Federal and feel our values in action. These events are also a story in and of themselves. They are a reminder of what Third Federal values as an institution, that we love, respect, and trust our associates. That we are all leaders who strive to give excellence to our communities and to ourselves as an organization.

The value of fun and the events and traditions that help reinforce that value have a very specific purpose. Not only do they reinforce our company culture, but they also let our associates know that they are valued and that they are a community. They break down the barriers between the leadership and the rest of our associates, giving us a culture of equality and cooperation. Fun also improves our productivity by keeping all of us happy, dedicated, and committed to the company.

Expectations are extremely high for our associates, so I am always itching to make things lighthearted. Fun, after all, is how people make their way in our culture. I'm the CEO who brought his overactive Great Dane puppy to work until the dog became too large to corral. I like to keep things light when other people might be hesitant to do the same.

Laughter is one of those natural by-products of fun that has a great practical purpose. It's a way of making new friends and connecting with old friends. It is a great stress reliever. I've heard that when President Reagan was shot, his cabinet and top aides gathered in the Situation Room of the White House, grimly facing the immediacy of the crisis. But when reports came in of Reagan saying he "forgot to duck," or asking his surgeons if they were Republicans, the worried team laughed out loud. The situation suddenly seemed more manageable.

Stories are vital to celebration and ritual, and stories are how family history gets passed along. It's an ancient pastime, and it's almost assuredly been a part of humanity since we gained the capacity for language. I've always had a particular love for Judaism and its stories and traditions, and I know that they are part of what has made the religion last for thousands of years. Sometimes I imagine ancient people standing at the city gates or walking to a neighboring homestead to discuss the news of the day or relate ancestral stories. Chatting was critical to passing along culture.

When nobody tells tribal stories, there's no historical context or reinforcing of values for the family or the community—there's no vitality in a society. It's how we make culture, and this means that storytelling isn't some waste of time. It's good for both the company and the individual. Stories can relieve tension, they pass time, and they let us address the things we care about: Who do we intend to be? What promises are we making to the world? What are we learning? What are we teaching? What's our legacy? The sociologist, Charles Tilly, wrote about the importance of the stories we tell ourselves. His book, *Identities, Boundaries, and Social Ties,* emphasizes the importance of the sharing of stories in order to create a sense of community, common purpose, and shared values.[33]

This practice is one I embrace. I encourage tribal storytelling whenever I can. I rarely miss an opportunity to tell a story about my father, my mother, or the experiences of the executives from the early days of Third Federal. As I've stated before, I encourage our associ-

33 Charles Tilly, *Identities, Boundaries, and Social Ties* (New York: Routledge, 2006).

ates to eat together, to spend extra time talking to customers. I like to sit down with associates to catch up with them. When we start telling each other stories, it might not be immediately evident that we're talking about the culture of Third Federal—the stories won't be so much about the "hows" of a family, business, or community but more about the "whys." Suddenly everything becomes personal; it isn't about facts like where we live and what we eat. It's about who we do those things with and what we learned about them.

If your stories are creating and reinforcing your culture, a job suddenly isn't just a place that you go to for a paycheck. It's part of your identity. Storytelling becomes a chance to reset the context and history surrounding the workplace. What, at another company, would just be a job, now becomes a desire to continue to participate in the culture, to help the company be successful to continue the history of that shared identity and make sure that it stays profitable and stable.

And storytelling is fun. It lets us feel things. We feel a sense of pride; we cry; we laugh.

Fun, for Third Federal, is profitable. It makes Third Federal a place where people can show their sense of humor, enjoy themselves, and know that they are part of something larger. Customers appreciate the happiness we have. Even over the phone, they know if an associate is enjoying the conversation. Having fun increases our creativity and enhances our communication.

The Origin of Fun

The evolution of implementing fun as a core value of Third Federal, perhaps ironically, followed a very structured approach.

When we were coming up with the idea of instituting core values at Third Federal, we did some research and discovered that the average adult smiles only fifteen times a day. So, "hey," we said, "let's try to do better than that at Third Federal." By the late 1990s, we created the Cabinet of Fun to reinforce the bank's core value of fun—having fun is serious business, it turns out.

In its time, the associates who made up the Cabinet of Fun made some real changes to the core of Third Federal. They targeted some of the more rigid traditions that had developed over the years. They started our cultural shift by reframing one of our big events—the annual officers-only meeting that began in my father's era. This was previously a pretty formal affair. We decided we would turn this on its head. We opened it up to all associates. We added music, skits, and humor, with their first effort featuring the senior management team dressing as a choir and entertaining attendees with holiday songs. Subsequent annual meetings became more raucous and eventually even featured fireworks, balloons, and confetti. It was a lot to clean up, but if your company culture needs a shift, you need to start big and move the needle. Otherwise, you'll find that your company falls right back into old habits.

It's also key to keep things innovative and new. Later in our effort to live up to the fun part of our values, we held a customer service rally that was deliberately baffling. We started with an exaggerated version of the way we had always started company meetings—with a longtime leader at the podium, this time giving what was a decidedly droning and methodical account of minute business concerns. We'd asked our speaker to keep to his script no matter what, and then we planted associates in the audience who feigned falling asleep with some very obvious telltale yawns and nodding heads. Just as it seemed like a good chunk of the audience was doomed to fall asleep, a local high school band crashed through the doors and everyone jumped out of their chairs. We continue to hold customer service rallies to renew our focus, but they haven't needed to be quite as wild now that we've shifted the culture toward expecting some fun. Having a pivitol event at the outset of a cultural change is an important moment, and we'd accomplished that.

As we continued to institute the value of fun, the associates came up with a score of ideas to promote happiness and satisfaction in the workplace. This was tailored for the specific audience in our company culture. Our associates, for instance, learned that some of us, including a certain not-to-be-named CEO, have a great love for magicians, illusionists, and sleight of hand artists—so there were plenty of those performers featured at our company functions—and we sometimes had them just drop by to liven up a lunch hour. The Cabinet of Fun also came up with a *Humor Handbook* that was in use for years. It was in the desk drawers of all the bank's team leaders in the effort to spread some light jokes around the company, and to remind their associates that these people, too, are human beings. Over time, these handbooks became so popular that they made their way around the company.

To this day, April is "Fun Month," and our associates are encouraged to wear team outfits. The crazier these are, the better, of course. Winter being what winter can be in Cleveland, we have broken the gloom by sometimes hosting special breakfast parties for Fat Tuesday where we provide paczkis (polish donuts), mimes, balloon artists, and caricature artists. Individual teams have donut-eating contests, summer ice-cream socials, and retirement celebrations.

I love being a part of our events. I suppose that comes from my garage band leanings. I'm the master of ceremonies at our associates-only winter meetings in Ohio and Florida. Not only is this part of my job as CEO, but I love these meetings, too, because they're the time of year when we introduce new associates to the culture of fun we have at Third Federal.

I call these new hires up before the crowd of their fellow associates. Usually, they sheepishly walk through the crowd and nervously ascend the stage. Often, I can tell that they're wondering why their CEO is in their face with his microphone, asking them light, but sincere, questions. It makes for great interactions— we've had people take the mic and do stand-up or sing with great talent—and it also does away with the stiff formality people expect from these meetings.

I also try to make time to visit at every table. I sit down and talk to the associates, let them know how much I care about them, and thank them for their dedication and loyalty. I also tell them that I hope that they're having fun and that I hope that they are working hard. And if they have any complaints, I'm there to hear them, if necessary. And usually no one complains, and everybody's pretty happy. It lets them get to know me. And to top it all off, this is considered work, so they're paid to have fun. After that all the fun has loosened people up and made them reflect on the fact that we are a family, we always talk for a few moments to discuss this message: working with each other at Third Federal is an honor, and it's a privilege to serve our customers, the people who trust us and keep us in our jobs.

We also plan appreciation events where families are welcome, and we even bus them in from distant offices. The families of our associates often remark how much they look forward to the get-togethers. I especially love it when my sons and daughters come back into town and join in on the festivities. I usually break out my keyboard and get the band back together. People have an image of a CEO that involves them being distant. You never see them. You never talk to them. They've got a corner office, and they hide out there making decrees. I try to be the antithesis of that, and one of the ways to do that is as a musician. And so having a musical show for everybody is a lot of fun and entertaining. It breaks down that invisible wall that some might imagine is there between myself and our associates. The audience is appreciative though thankfully not too discerning.

I would like to think that my father would approve of my making fun a core value for his bank. Times are different from how they were in his day, but we see real results that allow us to carry on the values he taught me.

Health Can Be Fun, and Health Is (Still) Wealth

As I've reflected in previous chapters, and as my father used to say "Health is Wealth." To that end, a lot of our fun at Third Federal is based around positive goals for our Third Federal Family. We have Commit to Quit, a smoking cessation program, and Commit to Fit, a wellness initiative. Commit to Quit participants can be rewarded for not smoking for an entire year. In the first year of the program, at least sixty associates quit smoking and earned a $1,000 reward. Meanwhile, the "Fit" associates received a cash stipend for a year's commitment to wellness and fitness. Many of these same people, almost twenty years into the program, still use the two fitness centers at our Corporate Campus, along with the locker rooms and outdoor track.

We have other fun activities that target support for the community, such as Jeans Day in which an associate can "purchase" the right to wear blue jeans to work by donating to a charity. Casual dress days don't include jeans, so this is special—so much so that I received a standing ovation when I announced it. We also have a company-wide focus on recycling in our facilities and among our associates, and, in the past, we have turned these into contests to see which floors or departments can do the most efficient recycling.

Part of health is psychological health, which is helped by having fun. The humor through the day cuts through stress and reminds us we are in a culture that sticks together and appreciates each other. When you embrace fun as a value and as something that creates health, it becomes the glue that holds things together. Being a community, ultimately, is different from being coworkers. Being a community requires that we create a culture that benefits all of us.

We want our associates to have fun on their own time, too, and we try to provide a strong foundation to enable that. Our salaries are on par with comparable banks, and we typically pay bonuses twice a year. Our vacation time is generous, and on each five-year anniversary of working for Third Federal, associates receive extra "appreciation days." Each Valentine's Day, I try to show appreciation to all our Third Federal associates in some way that will let them have more fun— whether that's through cards, candy, or some other small gift with a heartfelt letter. At the same time, every associate receives a meaning-ful contribution in their Associate Stock Ownership Program, our associate version of an Employee Stock Ownership Program. I also write cards for important anniversaries. These opportunities provide us more space for fun and make Third Federal a rewarding culture.

The more we have fun, and grow, and build ourselves together, the better off we all are. When associates work as hard as ours do, we support that hard work with a strong culture. When we break down the metrics by the number of associates at our bank, Third Federal closes three times as many first mortgage loans as the next competitor in the mortgage loan industry.

A Great Place to Work

In the late 1990s, I came across a magazine solicitation for the "*Fortune* One Hundred Best Companies to Work For." I felt like this was a designation that had been created just for us. Third Federal is a great place to work, and we've made it that way together. Over the years, the culture that we'd created with our values and our leadership had made a culture that anyone would enjoy working in. Day after day, I'd seen associates immensely enjoying themselves at work and forming a second family inside the organization, and I began to realize the impact our culture had created in every aspect of the business. In fact, we could gauge that impact by measuring just how successful our product introductions, branch expansions, and mortgage refinance rates were. We also had, and still have, a steady stream of referrals we gain from our satisfied customers.

I sensed that we deserved recognition. I wasn't sure if a small, Cleveland-based company could stand out in a nationwide competition. I wondered if maybe our culture was too personal and too unique to be captured in a magazine competition. I knew that the competition was focused on measuring aspects of the workplace—things like management credibility, job satisfaction, and camaraderie. I knew that efforts would be made to calculate those feelings and rank them as metrics and empirical measurements. But our workplace environment was, to my mind, immeasurable, since it is based around creating relationships and embodying our values, which, while it leads to great performance, isn't easily converted into pure math. I was also cautious because I was worried that it might have a deflating effect if we did well in the magazine competition. Some might feel we had finished our longtime hard work toward creating a unique working atmosphere at Third Federal and, feeling satisfied, might rest on our laurels.

Since I was unsure, I did what is usually the best option, and I presented the proposition to my management team. They were also taken in by the prospect, and they said that celebrating our values with some recognition from *Fortune* magazine would be a big victory and that it was important to them. They immediately took over my idea and made it their own. That was fine with me because, as CEO, I consider my leadership to be accomplished not just by standing in front but also by supporting from behind—and this was a time for me to lead from behind.

"Go for it," I said.

So we applied to the contest, which is run by the Great Place to Work Institute, a global organization with operations in forty-five countries. It partners with *Fortune* to publicize the results. The contest organizers sent out surveys to a random sample of Third Federal associates who were to submit their answers anonymously. Two-thirds of a company's score was based on the results of a Trust Index survey and one-third on the institute's culture audit.

Within a few months, we were informed that Third Federal was among *Fortune* magazine's top one hundred Best Places to Work in America. In fact, we made the top fifty among hundreds of applicants, including: such iconic companies as Whole Foods, Southwest Airlines, Starbucks, Microsoft, and Intuit. I was proud, and we had a small celebration where we handed out fortune cookies to everyone in the company.

In each of the five subsequent years, we steadily moved up the list, getting as high up as the fourteenth best place to work in America in 2005. Then the competition's rules were changed, and participation in the competition was limited to large companies. Since we were below 1,000 associates in those days, we could no longer participate. We have still, however, been ranked in several regional and national best workplace competitions since then.

Our associates weren't hesitant to carry the ball when it came to winning this recognition, and they deservedly took a lot of pride in our ranking. It also relieved me of the pressure to be the "take charge"

CEO or a high-energy captain to guide the effort. They were very capable of doing it themselves. That was reassuring because being a "take charge" guy isn't easy. Being a cheerleader is a little more up my alley, if truth be told. I was happy to let the team push forward.

Beyond the satisfaction of being recognized for our workplace culture, getting involved with the Great Place to Work Institute also benefited Third Federal's institutional knowledge because it gathered tons of information for the sake of the ranking. We received benchmark studies to compare our associates' responses with those of other companies. We were able to review where our associates considered us to be strong or weak.

It was a true joy to find that our associates placed us well into the 95 percent range when they rated our management style, benefits, fairness, and how fun and satisfying our workplace is.

In keeping with our commitment to being a great place to work, in 2019, Third Federal was named among the the Best Workplaces for Women and Best Workplaces in Financial Services and Insurance by *Fortune*. More important than the awards, however, are the values that make us win such accolades. We continue to focus on everything that makes us a "best workplace," whether or not we take the time to enter competitions.[34]

Fun Is Strong

Our values-focused institution leads us to outcompete the competition. We keep a lean, efficient team who can work harder and smarter because they truly know and value each other. Fun company events and our day-to-day culture constantly reaffirm our commitment to each other and to Third Federal itself.

---

34 Fortune, "Fortune 500 Past Ranking," accessed August 15, 2023, https://fortune. com/ranking/fortune500/pastranking.

Time and again, Third Federal's interest rate pricing has been the key to our success and to our competition's failure. And the secret of our pricing comes back to our culture and our lean, tight workforce. Analysts look behind Third Federal's customer-pleasing pricing strategy and see that our low operating costs allow us to establish these great rates. Our low operating costs can be tied directly to putting our money into our greatest asset: the payroll and benefits for our hardworking associates.

Our company's size is deceptive—we have one-third of the associates of banks of similar asset size. Third Federal's associates-to-assets ratios are much lower than comparable $17 billion financial institutions. Our small number of associates, which as of 2024 hovers around 1,000 people, produces the same results that other banks achieve with their much larger workforces. And our extremely low turnover rate, which I've mentioned is less than 5 percent annually, saves on hiring and training costs. Retaining associates for the long term also means that we have a bank made up of experts with superior skills and experience. That's hard to beat.

Third Federal's associates perform exceptionally well because Third Federal is a great place to work. It's a fun place to work. That gets the best work out of our associates, and it keeps us from having as much burnout as other companies. That makes us profitable.

It's all very simple in my mind. Happy associates make for happy customers—and happy customers make for better communities. In some ways, fun makes the world go 'round, and it's all too easy to forget that.

Music—A Parable about Balancing Fun and Excellence

Once there was a cricket who was exceptionally good at playing music. His songs drifted through the grass, attracting bugs from miles around to toss him scraps of food.

The cricket had been gifted since he was just a tiny nymph larva. He always sang for his meals and ate well.

The cricket had noticed that the days were growing shorter, and the nights a bit colder. The ants around him were hustling about their business, hauling great loads of chewed up mushrooms and shredded leaves. Seeing all that food, the cricket was hungry.

He began to sing.

A funny thing happened. Although creatures dropped scraps of food in front of him, almost nobody stopped to listen.

"Cricket," an ant said in the high, weedy voice that all ants share, "what are you doing? This is the season for saving and digging. Have you never seen a winter?"

The cricket, who had never seen a winter, was confused. "I don't need to dig. I'm Cricket. I play music. I'm the best at it. Everyone who hears my song feeds me."

"Music won't keep you warm when the frost comes. Start digging, Cricket." Her eyes were huge, and they reflected the gray sky and the bare branches overhead. "Do it now and you might be ok."

The cricket, who could only focus on his music, did not dig. He started another song, upbeat and heroic. This one always brought a lot of food.

The ant went back to digging.

Later, as winter fell, the cricket was indeed starving and cold. He tried playing his music. Nobody came.

He stumbled through the snow, his voice frozen. Suddenly, he fell, dropping through the snow and into the earth.

He was surrounded by ants, including the one whose warnings he'd ignored. They circled him. Cricket was nervous. Ants would eat anything. And Cricket was learning that winter was a desperate time.

"Cricket," she said, "we are great at digging. But we are tired. And you've broken our hive door."

Cricket started to sing. Something invisible passed between the ants, and they all bobbed in place a moment before returning to their work. The ant brought him a scrap of food.

"Sing to us while we work, Cricket. But just a short song. Then you help us dig. And you fix the door." The ant looked at him appraisingly. "You're huge. You'll make short work of it."

The cricket sang. He fixed the door. Then he went to dig himself a room. He was indeed good at it. There was a time to be great at singing and a time to be great at digging.

Adapted from *Aesop's Fables*

When I was a young manager near the beginning of my career, the city branch I managed was having trouble balancing their drawers at the end of the day. After trying many different tactics, I discovered that if I played some upbeat, funky music at the end of the day, we finished sooner and with fewer errors. Over time, I found that playing some unobtrusive music around the bank helped almost every operation go over more smoothly. It's something most of our branches still engage in to this day. A little fun was exactly what was needed to accomplish our goals, and the right balance brought us to our sweet spot. It's a philosophy that's done quite a bit for us.

> We must balance fun and work, but we can't do one without the other. Just as important, for our purposes, fun is often the ingredient that drives our culture, keeps us productive, shows that we appreciate each other, and breaks down barriers.

> Instilling any value is an ongoing process. It's constant—and it should be. A story that involves real people is never fully written. A culture is never fully formed in a way that won't change. Being a father, a CEO, and a leader is never-ending.
>
> And thank goodness for that.

Making a Difference:
A Legacy of Love

Dedicated to the One I Love

—THE MAMAS & THE PAPAS

Charity is one of the chief virtues of being a human being. We're at our best when we're helping others. It's always been my opinion that those who have the means to help others are under the obligation to do so. It's important to leave a legacy of love for our families and communities. Charity is a way of doing this that isn't just about making widgets.

*In memory of
Rhonda L. Stefanski,
August 6, 1957—
November 13, 2014.*

Starting with my father, my family has always done our best to contribute to our community. The Slavic Village neighborhood and the other areas surrounding our bank are some of the main areas in which we engage in community investment, but they're just the start of the impact of the Third Federal Way and our values.

One of the biggest impacts on our drive toward charity, and the namesake of one of the main charities of the Stefanski family, is

153

named for my wife, Rhonda, who passed away from pancreatic cancer in 2014.

I met Rhonda when I was in college. I was just a kid cleaning pools during the summer. She was hanging out by the pool, and my brother and I were working away when I spotted her. Despite the breach of professionalism, who am I kidding, I was a pool guy, I approached her and asked her out. Things fell into place pretty well, and we ended up spending the next forty years with each other before our life together was cut short.

Rhonda was one of the most caring people I'd ever met. She was the spirit of generosity. When it came to the holidays, she always had a gift for everyone—even when we stayed in a hotel, she had something for the staff. My children called her Mrs. Claus. She was extremely protective of families, and she wanted the best for everyone. She was an animal lover who gave often to animal-related charities. She made sure that everybody knew they were part of the same community and that we were there to support each other.

Rhonda was on the path to carrying out her own philanthropic undertakings when she was diagnosed with pancreatic cancer during a routine examination. Her efforts were cut short, as she passed away within ninety days of her diagnosis. It was quick and devastating for me and our five children.

After having seen the awful effects of cancer and knowing that Rhonda didn't get to carry out the biggest charitable endeavor she'd ever undertaken on her own, the Stefanski family started Rhonda's Kiss. This charity is aimed at bringing comfort and providing patient support services to those families who are undergoing cancer treatment and don't have the means to meet the various financial challenges a cancer diagnosis presents. As we learned there is quite a bit of funding for cancer research, but there is very little help for the patient support services people need while undergoing cancer treatment. Many families are not fortunate enough to be able to meet the challenges of fighting cancer and, at the same time, be able to pay nonhospital bills, and still care for their families. The thought of these people pains me, so our family decided that they would be the particular focus of Rhonda's Kiss. Our other established giving organizations, the Third Federal Foundation and the Stefanski Family Foundation were developed for a variety of other charitable endeavors, but Rhonda's Kiss would address a very specific need.

Rhonda's Kiss provides funds for its partner hospitals through events, awareness, and donation campaigns. The money funds grants at partner hospitals and can be used for the patient expenses other charities may not support—utility bills, car payments, groceries, home modifications, wigs, and especially transportation. These needs are expensive, and people deserve the dignity of having these things without sacrificing their healthcare or their well-being. It's an immediate, tangible benefit to people; it's the kind of thing my late wife would have adored doing for people. Her memory has had a positive impact on the world—at the time of writing this book, Rhonda's Kiss and the Stefanski family have been able to commit more than $2.5 million to its hospital partners.

One of my most cherished memories is of the first fundraising event held in Cleveland for Rhonda's Kiss. More than one thousand people attended, and we raised more than $600,000 in a single evening. I still remember the sight of people packed on the dance floor, having fun, and chipping in together to do something that mattered. The goodwill and genuine caring were something that you could almost feel in the air. It was the first time our entire family had gotten to gather since the loss of Rhonda, and the outpouring of love and community spirit made the event incredibly meaningful. After that resounding success, we made the event in Cleveland an annual affair, and it has been accompanied by events in Florida, Los Angeles, and New York City. True to my love of live music, the charity has been helped by many of the bands I grew up loving.

Aside from raising money for grants, these events remind the world that people care. And there's a great need for events like these. In 2019, cancer surpassed heart disease as the leading cause of death for middle-aged adults in the United States. As such diagnoses increase, so too does the need for charities like Rhonda's Kiss to provide help.

Rhonda's Kiss has partnered with numerous organizations, including Cleveland Clinic in Cleveland and Florida, University Hospitals in Cleveland, City of Hope and Cedars-Sinai in Los Angeles, and Brooklyn Maimonides Hospital in New York. Although hospitals administer funds through grants, I've learned the stories of some of the people we've helped as they, in turn, helped with events put on by Rhonda's Kiss after they went into remission. As a result of these events, the Cleveland Clinic was able to add dozens of patient navigators to its patient assistance programs, meaning that the number of patients who would be able to receive help was going to be multiplied by a large factor. These are stories that matter, stories about how Rhonda's Kiss helped people maintain their pride and dignity.

As part of Rhonda's Kiss, Third Federal also has an associate fund that is accessible to associates, and their families, when they are in need. This fund can cover medical expenses, financial needs, or other disasters that impact our associates. It's important that an organization takes care of people, whether that means customers, associates, or the surrounding community. The Rhonda's Kiss Associate Fund has been at the center of many important projects.

A story that stands out in my mind is one of the events that inspired the creation of the Associate Fund. This was a project that Third Federal undertook for one of our associates who was terminally ill. She was near the end of her life's journey, and she was bound to her house in a wheelchair. This woman loved her garden and had spent many years cultivating it. This situation had left her unable to access the garden she loved so much. We heard about this and found it unbearable. We worked toward building a ramp system in her home so that she would be able to spend the rest of her remaining time in her garden. Looking back on this memory, tending to patient support services that traditional insurance and medical charities do not cover is a vital cause.

As I mentioned previously, the Stefanski family is also involved with two other charitable organizations that serve different purposes. Rhonda's Kiss and the Associate Fund take care of cancer patients and Third Federal associates who need assistance. The Third Federal Foundation is aimed at helping the communities we serve. It specifically seeks out people and communities that are under-resourced, and is focused on community reinvestment. The foundation has helped with financial education and housing support services. The foundation distributes as much as $5 million in aid each year.

The Stefanski Family Foundation supports causes that are important to individual members of our family. This foundation grants $500,000 each year, usually to local organizations and causes.

Charity is deeply important to me. We humans need to be able to rely on each other, no matter how great or small of a difference we can make. If we don't help each other, who will? I'm once again reminded of Joe Ehrmann's insistence that being a true person of substance involves finding a cause greater than oneself. Involvement with my charities and the values of Third Federal are where I find this cause. I want to always be the young boy in the fable I refer to at the beginning of this book—the one who takes the time to throw stranded starfish back into the ocean, even if it's just to help one person. Because making a difference matters.

And it's something Rhonda would have loved.

If you're interested in helping the cause by participating in events or making a donation, you can visit **RhondasKiss.org** for more information.

Conclusion

Imagine

— JOHN LENNON

In 1999, Third Federal hired an analyst to look at our business. I wanted to make sure we were in great shape—to get an outside opinion. It's easy to miss something if you limit your perspective. They poked and prodded around the bank, getting to know the people involved, our processes, and how we managed our workforce. When finished, we sat down in my office and went over the big report at the end of their examination. They projected graphics, ran down the figures, and had generally dissected the entire business.

They were deeply impressed with how we do things. The results Third Federal gets are, after all, undeniable. But they had one nagging issue. Why not get rid of all the touchy-feely stuff? Why not eke out even more profit and productivity? Why not service customers faster? Why not expand more?

These are the kinds of questions I've come to expect from people who don't think the Third Federal Way. They put short-term profit over the core values we have, and it shows. Growth doesn't matter if it isn't stable. Profit doesn't matter if you need to exploit your customer, or your associates, to get it. That's how you lose good people. In our experience, that profit is likely to be destabilizing. Third Federal makes a profit by thinking in the long term. Our goal is always to be among the best in the market, and we do that by acting fairly and remembering our values.

It's also why Third Federal will be around long after many of these other, more exploitative, greedier businesses become bad memories. And we'll probably have the children and grandchildren of our current customers depositing their money with us.

This makes sense—Third Federal is, at the end of the day, a family business. In the way that I worked for my father, many Stefanskis have chosen to continue in the same tradition. They carry on the legacy that keeps customers coming back to Third Federal over the generations.

The love, trust, respect, commitment to excellence, and fun that drive the Third Federal Way make us exceptional. Adhering to all our values makes us a formidable force in the banking business. To find excellence, you need to love your customers and associates, to put their best interest at the heart of win-win relationships. You need your customers and associates to know that they can trust your institution, that they can rely on your business to do its best work. You need the respect for your community and everyone who makes up that community—a knowledge that people are good and want what's best for their families. You need to have fun to bring all these values together, to reinforce who your institution is, and what really matters to it.

If you can put together a great set of values, and you live them, you're creating a service that's bound to be better than your competitors. You'll be the place to which your customers bring their friends and family. You'll be the linchpin of a community, and you'll keep that community with you.

If you can develop a values-driven environment, your organization can find greatness. All the greatness you already have has almost certainly come from some combination of these ideas. That's why I live them, and that's why Third Federal lives them.

Mistakes Can Be Forgiven

None of what I've written is meant to say that you must be perfect to hold on to your values and put them to work; after all "perfect is the enemy of the good." Mistakes are very necessary for figuring out how your values work in the world and how you want them to.

As young men, my brother and I ran a pool cleaning service (yes, this would be the same cleaning service I was running when I met my late wife Rhonda). As the younger brother, I often took the subordinate role to my elder brother, who was more experienced in the field. One summer day, I was dispatched to clean the pool of an Ohio senator who had quite a bit of renown in our area, so I decided to work extra hard at that particular job. I wanted to impress the senator, just like most young guys probably would. I did all the usual cleaning steps with care. I scrubbed everything down and even used a pumice stone.

By the end of the job, I'd done every step of the water treatment, but I must have mismeasured something because I had some chemicals left over. I didn't want to dump them into the storm drain or leave them anywhere unsafe, so I decided to take the remnants over and dump them into what I thought was some open earth. I figured there was such a small amount of liquid that the dirt would just absorb it, and it would all be fine. Don't judge me too harshly here; it was the 1970s, and I was just a kid.

What I didn't notice was that there was a large, very old, exotic banyan tree not too far off from where I'd poured those chemicals. This was the kind of tree that grew in only one place on earth, apparently.

And that tree died shortly after this—right before a very big party the senator was having.

My brother, who was working at the house on the day everything came to a head, relayed the chaos to me. The senator was livid; his dead tree was going to leave a huge hole in the landscape of his party. The tree was beloved. He flew in an arborist, who was, forgive the pun, also stumped. I thought for sure that my goose was cooked.

I fessed up to my brother. He, of course, was not pleased. But when I shared the whole story with him, he circled back to a few facts: that I'd only been trying to do what I thought was safe and that I'd been in the predicament in the first place because I was working so diligently at getting the pool to a state of perfection.

He told me he'd handle it. And he did. All these years later, I'm not actually sure how, but we weren't fired, and he even helped pick up and plant the new tree.

My brother had mercy on me while also teaching me something— that sometimes, even when we're trying our best, we will fail. And that we learn from this failure and keep on. I've made a lot of high-minded demands of the people at Third Federal, but I never fault them for making a mistake, as long as that mistake wasn't a bad choice. I'd made mistakes on that day, but I hadn't made bad choices.

Choice comes into play when we know all the factors at work in a situation, and we do the wrong thing anyway.

If someone steals, or dissembles, or scams another person, they're making a choice (although such people are fond of saying they made "mistakes" if and when they get caught). These are things we know to be incorrect; they aren't done in the pursuit of being better.

As you integrate the values in this book into your life or company, try to forgive people their mistakes—and try to use these values to keep them from making bad choices.

Why We Shoulder Values

An experience that really hit home for me, and one of the events that put me on the path to writing this book, is also a fitting way to end this journey. I'd been thinking of these ideas for years, but the urge to share them really took shape when US Army General Stanley McChrystal came to visit Third Federal.

Stanley McChrystal was the four-star general who served as the commander of US forces in Afghanistan. He was heroic in his service in both Iraq and Afghanistan. He was instrumental in finding and eliminating Abu Musab Al-Zarqawi, the leader of al-Qaeda in Iraq, and for advocating the idea of the "surge" that helped the United States gain traction against the Taliban in Afghanistan. Even as he was undertaking this challenge, he was reputed to have run seven to eight miles a day, eaten only one meal a day, and to have slept only four hours each night. McChrystal is truly a figure out of a tall tale, so I was excited to bring him to Third Federal on a special visit.

Before he'd arrived, I'd read his memoir about his military leadership, *My Share of the Task: A Memoir*. McChrystal writes about what it takes to truly succeed in an environment where people are being pushed to their limits. He notes that success, whether in business or the military, takes a shared consciousness and a common purpose among those who are undertaking a task. He writes, "When [an organization is] faced with a problem and a landscape that is unknown, sharing informed perspectives across the organization builds a sense of common ownership and responsibility."[35]

This means that those inside of our organizations need to know each other, they need to share a perspective, and they need a common sense of what is important. The words struck me as important. They're

---

35   Stanley McChrystal, *My Share of the Task: A Memoir* (London: Portfolio Penguin, 2014).

the ideas I've always tried to hold on to with Third Federal. I invited McChrystal to come visit our campus in Cleveland.

He did indeed come and visit. It was an eventful day. I know that General McChrystal saw something he liked when he visited Third Federal, because he subsequently wrote me a note that read:

> Your focus on leadership is the core reason Third Federal is special.
>
> That became clear quickly. I was in awe of everything I saw and will never forget it. There is no better measure of true success than being able to make a difference.
>
> It is those acts we do when no one is looking that test the essence of the person.

There's a reason I opened this book with a discussion on leadership. Leadership—true leadership—is when we enact the values we want to see in the world. When we enact those values together, we're taking on a kind of collective leadership. We're choosing to make the lives of those around us better. All the associates at Third Federal lead together. We put people in homes. We provide credit to help build the world. We give people what they need to live their lives, and we often make them money while we do it. We help create communities and help keep those communities thriving. We share a common vision of the way the world should be, and we help each other to realize that dream.

The Gift of Kindness

As I write this, I've been reflecting on a new practice I've dedicated myself to—and preached heavily to my team. On holidays and special occasions, we've come to expect gifts—cards, objects, and money. Sometimes it's something a person really wanted; other times it might not be. Either way, I've realized that we rarely get what we want from these exchanges—the sentiment behind them. I'm now dedicated to giving people the gift of words. These can be kind, encouraging, loving, supportive, nurturing, or fun, but they'll definitely be words that are meaningful to the person I'm speaking to: "I love you;" "You're special to me;" "I couldn't run this company without you;" "You make a huge difference here."

The gift of kindness matters at home as well as at work. Imagine if we had more kind words for our significant others and friends and coworkers. The world could be changed.

All these sentiments mean a lot; they're powerful. It's not easy to forget harsh words; they leave an impact, so it's important that we make sure we're using kind words even more often. It's a path that provides something meaningful to those around me. Long after I am gone, I want people to remember me by my kind words and actions and the relationships that I nurtured. This is so much more important than any material possessions.

An awareness of how much people matter, of how we need to trust, love, and respect each other, and to have fun in our quest toward excellence, those are priceless things. They're the Third Federal Way.

I couldn't be more grateful for the chance to live my life the Third Federal Way.

I hope you have a chance to live that way too.

The Gift Horse—A Parable about Certainty

There was a little boy, and on his fourteenth birthday, he gets a horse.

Everyone in the village says, "How wonderful! The boy got a horse."

And the Zen Master says, "We'll see."

Two years later, the boy falls off the horse, breaks his leg, and everyone in the village says, "How terrible!"

And the Zen Master says, "We'll see."

Then, a war breaks out and all the young men have to go off and fight, except the boy can't because his leg is all messed up, and everyone in the village says, "How wonderful!"

And the Zen Master says, "We'll see..."

This story is one of the many reminders that we can't anticipate the future, that we don't know what's coming. I hope that the future brings all of us great things. None of us can control the outcomes.

But we can use our values to be patient, wise, and hardworking.

We can do our best and see.

My Playlist:

Forever Young —Rod Stewart

Happily Ever After (Now and Then) —Jimmy Buffett

In My Life —The Beatles

Clear Sailin' —Chris Hillman

Only to You —Richie Furay

The Family Tree —Venice

You've Got a Friend —Carole King

Let it Go —Zac Brown Band

Spellbound —Poco

Ships —Ian Hunter

Nobody Told Me —John Lennon

Carry Me —David Crosby

Sugar —Maroon 5

I Know You're Out There Somewhere —Moody Blues

Beautiful Boy (Darling Boy) —John Lennon

Over My Head —Fleetwood Mac

Can't Take My Eyes off You —Frankie Valli

Hold on —Wilson Phillips

Ride Captain Ride —Blues Image

Old Hat —The Sky Kings

You're the Best Thing That Ever Happened to Me —Gladys Knight

Run that Body Down —Paul Simon

Torn —Natalie Imbruglia

One of These Nights —The Eagles

Rock the Boat —Hughes Corporation

Favorite quotes:

"It is difficult to remove by logic an idea not placed there by logic in the first place." —**Gordon Livingston**

"If the map doesn't agree with the ground, the map is wrong." —**Gordon Livingston**

"Health is Wealth" —**Ben Stefanski Favorite**

"Who's got it better than us? Nobody!" —**Jack Harbaugh**

"Don't let it be forgot that there was a spot for one bright shining moment known as Camelot." —**Alan Jay Lerner**

Favorite Movie:

"It's a Wonderful Life"